The Dividend Investor

How to maximise your income by investing in shares

Rodney Hobson

HARRIMAN HOUSE LTD

3A Penns Road
Petersfield
Hampshire
GU32 2EW
GREAT BRITAIN

Tel: +44 (0)1730 233870
Email: enquiries@harriman-house.com
Website: www.harriman-house.com

First published in Great Britain in 2012
Copyright © Harriman House Ltd

The right of Rodney Hobson to be identified as Author has been asserted in accordance
with the Copyright, Designs and Patents Act 1988.

ISBN: 978-0857190-96-3

British Library Cataloguing in Publication Data
A CIP catalogue record for this book can be obtained from the British Library.

 Harriman House

Disclaimer

All the many case studies included in this book refer to genuine announcements and events on the London Stock Exchange. However, they represent the situation in each case at a given moment in time. Circumstances change and issues raised at one juncture may be resolved or superseded. Similarly, new challenges arise over time.

Therefore nothing in this book constitutes a recommendation to buy or sell shares in a specific company or sector. Investors must exercise their own judgement.

Readers interested in finding out more about a particular company should read the latest stock market announcements.

At the time of writing the author held shares in the following companies mentioned in this book: Royal Dutch Shell, Imperial Tobacco, Balfour Beatty, National Grid and Barratt Developments. These investments were made before this book was ever mooted and were being held for the long term. He holds a portfolio of shares in an ISA, built up over several years, which is designed to produce dividends.

eBook edition

As a buyer of the print edition of *The Dividend Investor* you can now download the eBook edition free of charge to read on an eBook reader, your smartphone or your computer. Simply go to:

http://ebooks.harriman-house.com/dividendinvestor

or point your smart phone at the QRC below.

You can then register and download your eBook copy of the book.

www.harriman-house.com

About the Author

Rodney Hobson is an experienced financial journalist who has held senior editorial positions with publications in the UK and Asia. Among posts he has held are news editor for the business section of *The Times*, editor of *Shares* magazine, business editor of the *Singapore Monitor* and deputy business editor of the *Far Eastern Economic Review*.

He has also contributed to the City pages of the *Daily Mail*, *The Independent* and *The Independent on Sunday*.

Rodney was at the forefront in the setting up of financial websites, first as head of news for the launch of *Citywire* and more recently as Editor of *Hemscott*, now part of Morningstar for whom he continues to write a weekly investment email. He has featured on BBC TV and radio and on CNBC, as well as having appeared as a guest speaker at conferences such as the World Money Show and the London Investor Show.

He is the author of *Shares Made Simple*, the authoritative beginner's guide to the stock market; *Small Companies, Big Profits*, a guide to investing in smaller quoted companies; *Understanding Company News*, the guide to interpreting stock market announcements; and *How to Build a Share Portfolio*, a practical guide to selecting and monitoring a portfolio of shares. All are published by Harriman House.

Rodney is registered as a Representative with the Financial Services Authority (FSA). He is married with one daughter.

Other books by the same author:

www.harriman-house.com/sharesmadesimple

www.harriman-house.com/smallcompaniesbigprofits

www.harriman-house.com/understandingcompanynews

www.harriman-house.com/howtobuildashareportfolio

Rodney Hobson's personal website is: www.rodneyhobson.co.uk

Contents

PART C – Investing Tactics | 113

Preface

Who this book is for

This book has been written for those who have grasped the basics of investing but are unsure as to how to build a portfolio of shares that will produce a steady and rising income.

However, investors of any experience should benefit from reading this book, irrespective of their investment criteria. Even those who have already built an investment portfolio and those who subsequently decide that they want to be active traders rather than stick to solid long-term investments will learn more about making the most of their capital.

Many investors plunge into shares with a vague notion of making money but without properly assessing what it is that they want from their investments. This book argues that regular income is a key part of any investment strategy, whatever the age or aspirations of the investor, and that shares are the best way of securing this income at relatively low risk and with the bonus of providing a hedge against inflation.

What this book covers

As the title implies, *The Dividend Investor* is all about buying shares for the income they generate through the dividends they pay their shareholders, as opposed to investing simply in the hope of returns from rises in share prices. The accent is on buying shares for the longer term rather than looking for quick fixes.

The focus is the UK stock market, although the arguments and guidance provided are relevant to all major stock exchanges around the world. The text refers mainly to larger and medium-sized companies because they are more likely to pay dividends than smaller ones. The concentration is on companies with a full listing rather than those quoted on AIM for the same reason.

The approach is practical rather than academic.

How this book is structured

The book is divided into four main sections: (Parts A-D) basic information on how dividends are set and by whom; how to analyse companies to maximise the yield on your investments; how to find companies that fit your investment criteria; and how to build your own portfolio using the knowledge that you have gleaned from the first three sections.

Chapters are arranged to lead investors step-by-step through the whole topic of investing for dividends. New and less sophisticated investors will particularly benefit from reading from start to finish. Even those with little knowledge of how the stock market works will feel competent to begin investing by the time they are half way through the book.

You can also use *The Dividend Investor* as a reference work. In particular, the chapters on the key figures and ratios that investors use to choose companies that fit their portfolios should be fully understood.

Supporting website

The accompanying website for this book can be found at: **www.harriman-house.com/thedividendinvestor**

Acknowledgements

Thanks for invaluable insights into how companies set and pay dividends are due to:

Paul Roberts, finance director, Wynnstay

Kulwant Singh, finance director, computer software supplier Delcam

Shatish Dasani, finance director, TT Electronics

Duncan Jeffery, marketing manager, Hargreaves Lansdown

and to Zoe Biddick and Katie Tzouliades of financial public relations company Biddicks.

Also thanks to Stephen Eckett of Harriman House for supplying extensive company data as well as for editing this book with his customary courtesy and perspicacity.

Introduction

Why dividends?

There are two major reasons for investing:

1. to produce income

2. to store wealth for some time in the future.

It is very important to recognise the remarkable power of dividends. Newspapers feed the public with daily doses of how share prices rise and fall, often commenting on how billions have been added to or wiped off the stock market or how shares in some company or another have gained millions in a single day because of one item of good news.

It is easy to be seduced by these dazzling figures that foster the notion that the stock market is all about making a fast buck in a gambler's paradise, especially in a bull market when all eyes are on rising shares prices.

In fact, the real money is made through solid investments that pay regular, rising dividends. The greater part of total returns for share investors over time will come from dividends, not capital gains. And when markets are falling, your only gains are likely to come from dividends.

To demonstrate the importance of dividends we can look at figures produced by the Barclays Equity Gilts Study, which showed that £1,000 invested in shares at the end of the Second World War would have been worth £57,210 by the end of 2009.

However, had we reinvested the dividends our pot would have ballooned to a massive £924,600.

So unless you are a very short-term trader, you should be investing for dividends as part of any strategy for capital growth. Companies paying gradually improving dividends are the ones that will see their share price rise over time and the income from dividends will help to offset any capital losses you may suffer.

Even short-term investors should consider running a separate long-term investment portfolio as a back-up. Therefore almost every investor should be a dividend investor.

It is possible to invest by putting your money into a fund such as an investment company or trust. You can find out how to do this in chapter 24. However, you are abrogating responsibility for your finances to a fund manager who cannot possibly know what you want from your investments and what risks you are prepared to take.

The performance of individual funds can vary enormously from year to year. The one constant is that the manager has to be paid out of *your* money. There is absolutely no reason why you cannot make sensible investment choices yourself, retaining control of your own destiny. Even if you do not perform quite as well as the fund manager, you will come out ahead because you are not paying the fund's fees.

With the help of this book you can compete easily with the City professionals, retaining the flexibility to invest as, when, and where you choose.

PART A

Dividend Basics

Chapter 1
Companies and Dividends

The purpose of companies – to pay dividends

Let us be quite clear: the whole purpose of companies is to pay dividends. It goes like this:

1. a company is set up

2. the company makes a profit

3. the owners share the profit

4. we all live happily ever after.

The payment of dividends is, or should be, the *raison d'être* of all companies whose shares are quoted on any stock exchange. Dividends are the reward paid to shareholders who have invested their money in the business.

Yet in a sense dividends come last in the pecking order. They are funded out of what is left over after a whole range of bills and obligations have been met, such as:

- staff wages
- trade creditors
- tax
- interest and repayments on bank loans
- pension fund contributions
- bondholders
- cash to meet day-to-day needs (working capital)
- investment in the company.

There are two factors that affect whether a dividend is paid at all:

1. The company must have made a profit, either in the current or in previous years.

2. The company must have some cash to fund the dividend.

Companies do not normally pay out all the profits as they arise. Some cash is retained to fund the day-to-day operations of the company and some is held to fund expansion or new plant and machinery. Profits that are thus retained in the business build up in what are known as 'distributable reserves', so called because this is the amount of cash that can legally be distributed to shareholders in dividends.

If the company makes a loss, that will reduce the size of the distributable reserves. If losses persist and all the distributable reserves are used up, the company cannot pay dividends. Any accumulated losses must be fully offset by subsequent profits before the dividend can be restored unless the company receives permission from the High Court for a capital restructuring.

Cash is king

To emphasise, the company must actually have cash available to pay dividends. Profits on paper are no use in this respect. Your house may be worth twice as much as you paid for it but you cannot spend any of that gain unless you actually sell it. Similarly companies may make profits on paper, say from the revaluation of assets, but cash is king.

These rules apply to all companies, irrespective of their size or sector. You may find that companies with heavy capital costs, such as manufacturers and plant hire companies, build up larger distributable reserves to conserve cash. Companies with erratic profits will also want to keep sizable reserves so that they can maintain a steady dividend in good years and bad.

In contrast, companies with strong cash flow and low debts will find it easy to dish out the dosh.

Dividends can grow even in hard times

Total dividends paid by UK quoted companies actually grew in 2008, after the scale of the credit crunch had become only too apparent, to £67.1 billion from £63.1 billion in 2007. That is a lot of money for non-investors to be missing out on.

Admittedly, dividends were scaled back in 2009, to £58.4 billion, and again in 2010 to £56.5 billion. However, the fall in 2010 was entirely due to the suspension of BP's dividend for the first three quarters of the year, according to figures compiled by Capita Registrars, which keeps the shareholder records of well over 1,000 quoted companies up to date.

Companies apart from BP increased their dividends by an average of 7.5% in 2010 as their shareholders received an early boost from the nascent economic recovery.

Even better was to come, for in 2011 UK-quoted companies paid £67.8 billion in dividends, more than they had ever handed to shareholders in any one year.

It is true that Capita's data showed a heavy dependence on a few dividend payers. For instance, in 2010 just five very large companies – Shell, Vodafone, HSBC, GlaxoSmithKline and AstraZeneca – paid 38% of total dividends, while the top 15 companies paid 61% of all dividends.

So anyone investing in the largest companies would have received solid dividend payments notwithstanding the misfortune at BP, which in any case restored its dividend, albeit at a lower level, in the final quarter of 2010.

Spreading investments without increasing risk

However, there was plenty of scope for investors to spread their investments much more widely without significantly increasing risk because:

1. Fund managers invest disproportionately in the largest companies, leaving many medium-sized and smaller companies undervalued and offering higher yields.

2. The credit crunch left larger companies paying a disproportionate percentage of total dividends, a distortion that would be addressed as smaller companies came through the economic squeeze.

3. It is smaller, not larger, companies that bounce back soonest and furthest in the early period of recovery.

As Table 1.1 illustrates, smaller companies sensibly conserved cash and reduced debt in the immediate aftermath of the credit crunch. Soon, however, they were returning to paying dividends and taking up the slack caused by the fall in the BP dividend. Thus the top dividend payers were responsible for a declining proportion of the total paid.

Table 1.1 – Company size profile of UK dividend payers

Year	Total dividends	Top 5	Top 15	The rest
2009	£58.4 billion	45%	67%	33%
2010	£56.5 billion	38%	61%	39%

More data from Capita reinforces this point: dividends from the medium-sized companies in the FTSE 250 Index rose 16.3% in 2010 while those from the FTSE 100 increased by only 6.8% (and it should be said that for investors to see their income rise by 6.8% in one not particularly promising year shows the potential benefits of dividend investing).

The trend continued. In particular, manufacturing companies that had struggled to remain competitive with cheaper production areas in Asia and Latin America rebuilt profits as the falling value of the pound on the foreign exchange markets gave UK exporters an edge.

Companies as diverse as ceramics specialist Cookson, which had not paid a dividend since the middle of 2008, and aviation services and newspaper distribution group John Menzies returned to the dividend lists early in 2011.

How is the size of dividend decided?

Technically the size of the dividend is decided by the shareholders in a vote at the Annual General Meeting (AGM). Interim dividends, decided by the board of directors, can be paid during the course of the year but the final dividend is not paid until approved by the AGM.

The agenda for the meeting may include a motion for shareholders to confirm any interim dividends already paid and to approve a final dividend recommended by the directors. Often, however, the dividend is not even mentioned on the agenda and shareholders are simply asked to approve the report and accounts, which includes details of the dividends.

It is clearly impossible to try to vote down the interim dividend and attempt to claw the money back from shareholders, some of whom will have subsequently sold their shares, although in theory the proposed final dividend could be rejected.

In reality, the board of directors decide on a figure for the interim and final dividends and this recommendation is nodded through by the shareholders.

As Table 1.2 covering AGMs held in 2011 shows, the dividend is almost invariably passed by a very large majority even where shareholders express their disquiet over, or openly revolt against, an issue such as directors' pay.

Table 1.2 – Sample shareholder votes at company AGMs

Company	Remuneration report – votes for (million)	Remuneration report – votes against (million)	Dividends – votes for (million)	Dividends – votes against (million)
Shell	3,237.8	40.5	3,373.2	1.7
HSBC	6,652.1	1,533.9	8,402.6	121.8
Betfair	63.9	2.7	66.6	0.1

In fact, for such a major matter there tends to be very little debate of any kind over the dividend. Although boards of directors meet every month, the dividend will be on the agenda only twice a year (or four times if there is a quarterly dividend) and then probably only as an item among the half-year or full-year results.

The finance director (sometimes called the chief financial officer) will draw up the results to be presented to the board and will suggest the size of dividend that is justified by the results. He or she will take into consideration:

- the amount of profit that has been made in the relevant period

- how much cash the company has in hand

- the level of company debt, in particular whether any debts are due to be repaid

- the amount of capital spending required in the current financial year

- the extent to which income covers interest payments on debt

- whether the company has a policy of maintaining or increasing the dividend each year.

Because these are all financial matters, the view of the finance director on what the level of dividend should be is of considerable importance and he or she will almost certainly have a figure in mind. This proposed dividend will usually be discussed with the chief executive, and possibly the chairperson, ahead of the board meeting to see if there is a broad agreement among these key directors.

The finance director's proposal will be put to the board meeting and if there is no alternative suggestion then that is that. If the chief executive feels strongly that a different amount is appropriate then a second proposal will be put to the meeting for debate and a vote will be taken on the rival amounts. In the event of a tie, the chairperson's casting vote will decide.

Very often there is no debate, and any discussion would almost always be reasonable and courteous, however good or bad the results. A heated row is highly unlikely and would happen only if the results are disastrous and the dividend has to be reduced or suspended.

In the end, most dividends are agreed unanimously. The scope for manoeuvre is limited by the parameters set by the results.

One item that may be discussed is whether to rebalance the dividend. Sometimes a company may be cautious after the first half and hold down the interim dividend; if all goes well the final dividend can be raised. Thus the final dividend may become disproportionately large compared to the interim. In such a case the board may debate raising the interim dividend by a larger amount than the final to bring the ratio between the two dividends into line with the generally accepted norm of 33:67.

Case study: Wynnstay

According to Paul Roberts, the finance director of Wynnstay, the most important point in setting the dividend is to maintain balance.

His company, supplying agricultural products and pet foods, was floated on the Alterntive Invesrtment Market (AIM) in 2004 after two years on Ofex, the third tier trading system now called Plus. By August 2011 it had a stock market capitalisation of £54.5 million.

Initially it paid just one, final, dividend a year to keep down costs but introduced an interim dividend in 2006, roughly in the ratio of 1:2.

As the man in charge of the coffers, Paul is conscious of the need to retain sufficient cash to develop the business while providing some rewards for shareholders.

He says:

> We have had a long term strategy, both prior to flotation and since, to give a clear view to the markets what our dividend policy would be. Because we are a small cap company we have a requirement for capital so retained earnings are an important part of our strategy. However, the message that we put out was that the dividend policy would be progressive, all other things being equal.

The directors were conscious that larger companies usually try to cover the dividend two or at most three times with earnings but Winnstay made it clear from the start that it would probably be targeting a higher dividend cover policy. The board felt a cover of about four times was appropriate.

Paul says this openness has been well received by the stock market – indeed some shareholders indicated that they would be willing to forego dividends in the early years to allow more cash to be invested in the company.

However, Wynnstay has stuck to its intention of increasing the dividend by 5-10% each year since it changed its financial year from the calendar year to the 12 months to 31 October in 2006.

Table 1.3 – Historic dividend payments by Wynnstay

	2005-6	2006-7	2007-8	2008-9	2009-10
Dividend (p)	5.25	5.5	6	6.5	7.1
Increase (%)	5	4.8	9.1	8.3	9.2
Cover (x)	3.2	3.4	4.85	4.1	3.9

Paul says:

> The dividend virtually sets itself. If we were unable to extend the dividend by the expected amount we would probably find it necessary to give an explanation to the market.

He says that the board effectively only has to decide the odd decimal point in the dividend level and "there is rarely a big discussion". As finance director he has an understanding of what the market is expecting and proposes what the dividend should be, possibly after chatting to senior colleagues, before presenting the results to his fellow directors.

Different types of dividends

Besides straightforward cash dividends (which is the main topic of this book), there are some other types of dividends – which are briefly described below.

Scrip dividends

Many companies offer you the opportunity to take your dividend in the form of more shares in the company rather than cash. This is known as a 'scrip dividend'. The company will say in its results announcement whether it offers a scrip dividend.

Not all companies offer this option and it may not be available to you if you run an online account where shares are held in a nominee account. Check with your broker whether you will be able to elect to receive scrip dividends.

Basic rate income tax will still be deducted from the dividend before the number of scrip shares due to you is calculated according to the level of the cash dividend and the stock market value of the shares. New shares will be issued accordingly.

If, as is likely, the amount of the dividend is not divisible exactly by the share price and there is a fraction of a share left over, the difference is – depending on the particular terms of the scheme – paid to the shareholder, added to the next dividend, retained by the company, or given to charity.

If scrip dividends are issued to a company in your ISA account, the new shares qualify for tax relief under the ISA scheme.

Scrip dividends *are* attractive if:

- You want to build up your investments.

- You have a range of investments and are not looking to diversify into more companies.

- The company is doing very well and you are happy to keep on investing in it.

- You do not consider the shares to be overpriced.

Scrip dividends *are not* attractive if:

- You want income to live on now.

- You want to widen your portfolio.

- Your portfolio is already weighted too heavily in shares in this particular company or the sector it operates in.

- You feel that there are more attractive prospects elsewhere.

Dividend reinvestment plans

If a company you invest in does not offer scrip dividends, it may still be possible to take dividends in shares through a dividend reinvestment plan, known as a DRIP – an appropriate acronym not because dividend reinvestment plans are stupid, but because they allow you to drip more shares into your investment pot.

The difference between a scrip issue and a DRIP is that no new shares are issued with a DRIP. Instead, participants in the scheme have their cash dividend paid directly to the scheme administrator, which is usually the company's registrar. The administrator then calculates the number of shares to which each participant is entitled and buys the shares on the stock market. Shares are then distributed to the participants.

The administrator will obtain the best price it can for the purchase and because the share purchases can be aggregated, the dealing costs tend to be relatively low.

The arguments for and against DRIPs are exactly the same as for scrip dividends. If you elect to take scrip dividends where possible you will almost certainly be keen to take advantage of DRIPs as well. DRIP shares issued into an ISA account remain within the ISA wrapper just as scrip dividends do.

A list of companies that have a DRIP scheme can be found on the Equiniti share registrars website at:

www.shareview.co.uk/Products/Pages/applyforadrip.aspx

Where companies offer neither a scrip dividend nor a DRIP, your stock broker may offer a dividend reinvestment scheme, automatically reinvesting the cash dividend into the relevant company's shares. Again, the arguments for and against are the same as for scrip dividends and again any shares issued in this way remain part of an ISA.

Some brokers lump together dividends paid to several clients holding shares in the same company and buy new shares immediately. Others wait until cash builds up in each individual client's account before buying. Aggregating cash in this way reduces dealing costs.

When you set up an online account you will be asked whether you want to have dividends remitted to your bank account or retained within the investment account. If you want your dividends to be reinvested automatically, check that this option is available, otherwise find another online broker.

If you are operating a traditional account with your broker, ask if this option is available.

Special dividends

Occasionally companies will pay a special dividend. This is a one-off payment in addition to the normal interim and final dividends but, unlike the regular payouts, it will not be repeated the following year.

A special dividend usually arises when a company has sold some assets for cash and has no obvious way of using that money to expand the business. Another possibility is that the company has retained large sums of cash from previous profits, possibly to finance a planned acquisition that never materialised, and has finally decided that there is no point in hanging on to the money.

One should not look a gift horse in the mouth and it is right that this money should be handed out to shareholders who do, after all, own the company and all its assets including cash.

A special dividend does imply that the company is on a sound financial footing and that regular dividends are secure for the foreseeable future, otherwise the company would shore up the balance sheet or keep the cash in reserve to maintain regular dividends.

On the other hand, if the company has sold assets its earnings may be reduced in future. Another negative view could be that if the company is returning cash to its shareholders then this suggests the directors are lacking in ideas of how to grow the company. You need to look at the circumstances and decide.

Whatever the reason for the special dividend, remember that it is a one-off payment and that dividends are likely to return to normal the following year.

Dividends declared in foreign currencies

Foreign-based companies and those with overseas operations may declare their results in a foreign currency, most likely US dollars or euros. This can make sense if most of their income and expenditure is priced in that currency.

Some UK companies present their results in dollars, particularly those in the oil industry or mining, where products are priced in the American currency.

European companies will normally declare their results in euros, although they may use pounds if their shares are listed in the UK. Otherwise the international currency is the US dollar.

The dividend will still be paid to you in pounds sterling but the amount will depend on the prevailing exchange rate. It follows that dividends from these companies tend to be more erratic as exchange rates fluctuate. When the value of the pound falls you do better; when the pound rises your income is reduced.

Another drawback is that foreign companies will operate within different political and legal systems. This is particularly relevant if you choose an overseas company with its shares quoted on AIM, where the regulatory framework is less rigorous.

Nevertheless, a willingness to invest in companies declaring their results in dollars or euros will widen your potential range of investments and spread your risk.

Key points

- To be able to pay regular dividends a company must generate profits and cash.

- Dividends are in effect paid out of what is left over after all other commitments have been met.

- The dividend is decided by the board of directors, usually following the recommendation of the finance director.

Chapter 2
The Dividend Timetable

Payment frequency

Dividends are normally paid twice a year but they may be paid four times a year or, more rarely, once a year.

Frequency of payment is not particularly important in itself as long as the company maintains a regular pattern. If you want dividends to live on, then companies paying four times a year give you a smoother flow of income.

However, finding companies making steady, reliable profits is more important than looking for ones that make more frequent payouts.

Once-a-year dividend payments

This is extremely rare. A company making just one annual payment is probably very small and is trying to save money by reducing administrative costs. You should be more cautious of such a company as you will want to be satisfied that it has adequate financial resources.

Most dividend investors would prefer a steady stream of dividends throughout the year rather than have them lumped together, although having just one company that pays a single dividend in your portfolio should not be too much of a distortion overall.

One point to bear in mind is that other investors will be wary of such companies so they may be comparatively cheap to buy.

Twice-a-year dividend payments

This is the norm for the UK. One dividend, the *interim dividend*, is paid after the half-year results are announced. The second dividend, the *final dividend*, is paid after the full-year results are in.

Table 2.1 gives some examples of companies with financial years to the end of March 2011 paying two dividends a year.

Table 2.1– Sample dividend payments for UK companies

Company	Interim	Final	Total
Johnson Matthey	12.5p	33.5p	46.0p
Marks & Spencer	6.2p	10.8p	17p
Vodafone	2.85p	6.05p	8.9p

In each case the final dividend is substantially higher than the interim although the proportions vary. Retailer Marks & Spencer's interim is more than half the size of the final while telecom giant Vodafone's is just under half and chemicals group Johnson Matthey is closer to a 1:3 ratio.

Four-times-a-year dividend payments

International companies such as oil majors and pharmaceutical groups are more likely to pay quarterly dividends, as are foreign-based companies. Quarterly accounts are the norm in the United States so you will often find that companies producing their results in US dollars rather than sterling pay quarterly dividends.

These companies sometimes refer to the final dividend as the *fourth interim dividend*. If you see an interim dividend declared for the fourth quarter, do not expect another, final, dividend on top. It has been called an 'interim dividend' so that it can be paid without waiting for the approval of shareholders at the AGM.

Table 2.2 gives examples of companies paying four dividends a year.

Table 2.2 – Sample dividend payments for UK companies

Company	Q1	Q2	Q3	Final
Barclays	1p	1p	1p	2.5p
HSBC	8 cents (5.32p)	8 cents (5.05p)	8 cents (5.2p)	10 cents (7.25p)
Royal Dutch Shell	42 cents (27.37p)	42 cents (26.89p)	42 cents (26.72p)	42 cents (25.82p)

These three companies all have international operations including interests in the United States. Two of them, one bank(HSBC) and one oil company, declare their results and set their dividends in US dollars while Barclays retains its Britishness with results and dividends in sterling. The figures given are for the 2010 calendar year.

We can see that they each have a different attitude to how the dividend should be split between the four payments:

- Barclays has decided to make the final dividend more than double the size of each of the three interim dividends.

- HSBC has a higher final dividend than the interim dividends but one that is only 25% greater than each interim.

- Shell makes four equal payments – in this instance changes in the £/$ exchange rate meant that the final dividend was lowest in sterling terms.

How dividends are weighted between interim and final

There are no hard and fast rules as to how much of the total dividend should be paid at the interim stage and how much should be held back for the final.

Some companies, such as package holiday suppliers and some retailers, depend heavily on a particular time of year. They tend to put the better trading period into the second half, thereby seeing the results for the full year before deciding on the size of the final dividend.

As a rough guide, companies making two payments a year tend to pay one-third of the total at the halfway stage and two-thirds at the final stage. Companies paying four dividends a year usually spread the payments more evenly and may actually make four equal payments.

One should not draw inferences from the differing policies regarding the weighting of the dividend. What matters is that the company pays them, and pays according to a consistent policy year by year.

When you get paid

Dividends are not paid immediately the accounting period ends. It can be several months before you get your money. Table 2.3 covers five companies picked at random from those with a financial year ending on 31 December.

The list is in order of the announcement, in early 2011, of the full-year results for 2010. The dividend referred to is the final dividend.

Table 2.3 – A sample of key dividend dates

Company	Results announced	Ex-dividend	Date on register	Dividend paid	AGM
Shell	3 February	9 February	11 February	25 March	17 May
BAT	24 February	9 March	11 March	5 May	26 April
HSBC	28 February	16 March	17 March	5 May	27 May
Cookson	1 March	18 May	20 May	6 June	12 May
John Menzies	8 March	25 May	27 May	24 June	20 May

Source: Individual company announcements

With reference to Table 2.3, some notes follow on each column.

1. Results announced

We can see first of all that there was a gap of more than a month between the first and the last results announcement. Larger companies tend to produce results more quickly than smaller ones as they have a larger and more experienced financial staff.

Each company tends to produce its results on pretty much the same day each year, give or take a week, so we should not worry unduly unless results fail to appear at the normal time. As a general principle, any delay in producing results is likely to be because of particularly bad news.

2. Ex-dividend

The second date shows when the companies go ex-dividend (often abbreviated to *ex-div*). Buy before this date and you are entitled to the dividend that has been announced. Buy on or after this date and you are not entitled to the dividend.

The ex-dividend date is always a Wednesday. While in theory it could be any day of the week, there is some advantage to investors in knowing that the cut-off point is always the moment that trading closes on Tuesday evening. After that it is too late to buy for the latest payout.

While several newspapers publish each Monday a list of companies due to announce results in the coming week, a comprehensive list of those going ex-div is not so readily available. You will probably find that the Reuters website is the most convenient way to check. Access to this page is free.
http://uk.reuters.com/business/markets/dividends

On the day that shares go ex-dividend the share price will usually fall by roughly the same amount as the dividend to reflect the fact that new share buyers will not receive the dividend.

Table 2.4 shows three companies from different sectors that all went ex-dividend on 17 August 2011.

Table 2.4 – Sample of share price moves when companies go ex–dividend

Company	Sector	Dividend	Close 16 Aug	Open 17 Aug	Change	Close 17 Aug	Change on day
BAT	Tobacco	38.1p	2,784p	2,737.5p	- 46.5p	2,738.5p	- 45.5p
Pearson	Media	14p	1,099p	1,080p	- 19p	1,072p	- 27p
Prudential	Insurance	7.95p	636.5p	625p	- 11.5p	621p	- 15.5p

Source: Company announcements

The FTSE Index fell 30 points on that day, about half of 1%, after a weak opening so we would have expected shares going ex dividend to lose slightly more than the amount of the dividend.

We can see that all three shares opened lowed than we would have expected, all things being equal – that is, they all fell by more than the dividend to which share buyers were no longer entitled. This reflected weak stock market conditions. Pearson and Prudential continued to give ground during the day although BAT began to buck the trend, recovering just 1p during the course of the trading day.

3. Date on register

Dividends are sent to those who appear on the share register on this date, which always falls on a Friday two days after the ex-div date to allow time for the register to be updated with all deals done cum dividend.

Do not worry if you buy or sell shares on the Wednesday or Thursday. The share registrar will know whether shares have been bought or sold cum or ex dividend.

If you bought cum (with) the dividend you are entitled to it; if you bought ex (without) then it is not yours but if this worries you, just do not buy or sell shares around the ex-dividend date.

The date on register is always Friday for historical reasons. The London Stock Exchange used to have two-week settlement periods. On alternate Fridays all the deals of the previous two weeks were processed. So all deals done cum dividend were processed on the Friday and shareholders entitled to the dividend were on the register that day.

With the arrival of electronic trading all deals are now settled and processed in two days. The Friday register day has remained but the ex-dividend date has moved closer to it to allow for the shorter settlement and processing period.

4. Dividend paid

You may think that there is absolutely no reason why the cheques or transfers cannot go out first thing Monday morning, and you would be quite right, but alas there is further delay before you get the money that is rightfully yours.

The company arbitrarily sets a date on which the dividend is actually paid. As with all the other dates in this equation, the interval can vary considerably.

For instance, although Cookson takes a full two months to announce its annual results and a further two-and-a-half months to go ex-dividend, its dividend payment date is just two-and-a-half weeks later. BAT can get its results out in less than two months and goes ex-dividend only two weeks later but it takes nearly two months to actually shell out.

There is no logical reason why any company should delay the payment of dividends once they are announced. Those that do so tend to be somewhat defensive if you raise the issue.

They normally argue that as long as the dividends come round at regular intervals, that is all that matters to shareholders. The company is making good use of the money in the meantime, they say.

Once we finally reach the dividend paid date, it can still take a few days before your money is actually in your bank account, even in this electronic age.

There are two methods of payment: through the Bankers' Automated Clearing Services (BACS) system, where you are paid automatically into your bank or stockbroking account, or by cheque.

You may have no choice in the payment method. Most accounts and virtually all online accounts are arranged so that dividends are transmitted into your stockbroking account by BACS and, if you have asked for the cash to come to your own bank account, will be transmitted onwards by your broker, also by BACS.

Check with your broker when you set up your account what the payment method will be.

There are several advantages of being paid by BACS:

- The dividend is transmitted from the registrar on the payment date and should appear in your own bank or stockbroking account within a couple of days.

- There is no chance of the payment being delayed in the post.

- You do not have to wait for a cheque to clear.

- This payment method is more secure than receiving a cheque through the post.

- If you move house, payments will not be directed to your old address.

How time flies

All in all, there can be a considerable delay between a company's financial year end and the day when the dividend is actually in your account. The time difference can vary enormously. Among our examples, Shell pays fairly quickly but even so it is nearly three months after year end and seven weeks after results are announced before the cash reaches your account. This is about as fast as it gets.

Cookson pays a full five months after year end and three months after the results announcement; for Menzies the gap is nearly six months from year end.

5. The AGM

Finally, we note the varying attitudes towards the AGM. Shell and HSBC do not even bother to wait for shareholder approval before making the final payment for the year. In an exercise in semantics, they call the final dividend the 'fourth interim dividend', so technically there is no final dividend for shareholders to approve.

BAT goes for a halfway house, with the AGM after the ex-dividend date – like Shell and HSBC – but before the payment date. BAT asks shareholders to approve the report and accounts without specific reference to the dividend.

Cookson and John Menzies both seek approval from shareholders before the ex-dividend date and both have a resolution to approve the final dividend on the AGM agenda.

Timing your income

If you want to receive dividends to live on or to supplement your pension then you would naturally prefer to receive a roughly similar amount each month.

Alas, this feat is virtually impossible (see Figure 2.1) and you should not attempt to pick investments on the basis that a particular company pays a dividend in a month where you are a bit short of the readies. Choose the best prospects, even if that makes your income lumpy.

Spreading the dividends you receive is difficult because:

- Most companies have year ends at 31 December or 31 March.
- Retailers usually have financial years running to the end of January, adding to the bias towards announcing full-year results in the early part of the year.

- Very few companies apart from holiday operators have year ends in the autumn.

- You are likely to have different sizes of holdings in your portfolio and in any case companies pay different sizes of dividends.

As I have noted, some companies take longer to pay the dividend than others, which will help to spread your income a little more evenly, but you have to accept the fact that you will not have the same amount coming in each month.

But then, nor will your outgoings be the same each month. While day-to-day items such as food and clothing can be spread fairly easily, energy costs will be higher in winter and holiday spending higher in summer. Always give yourself a little leeway in terms of keeping some ready cash available.

Figure 2.1 illustrates the distribution of final dividend payment dates throughout the year for the 618 companies in the FTSE All-Share Index.

Figure 2.1 – Distribution of dividend payment dates for FTSE All-Share companies

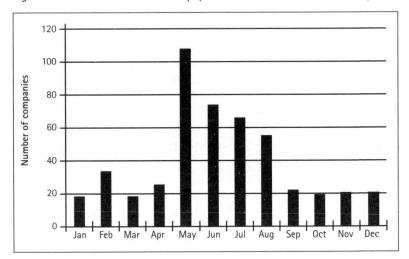

As can be seen, final dividend payment dates are clustered in the period May–Aug, with the most popular month being May, when 109 companies paid their dividends (which largely reflects the fact that the overwhelming majority of companies have their financial year ends between 31 December and 31 March). From this, we can see that if one holds a reasonably diversified portfolio of FTSE All-Share companies, the (final) dividend income is going to be concentrated in the May–Aug period.

Interim dividends tend to be concentrated around the calendar year end.

Key points

- Income from dividends will be lumpy with the bulk of payments coming in mid-year and a grouping of interim payments around year-end.

- Do not try to smooth out income by investing in a company just because it makes payments in spring and autumn.

- Do not worry if a company takes longer than others to pay the dividend – what is important is that it is a sound investment and it pays dividends at the same time each year.

Chapter 3
Where to Find Information

Company news

One of the great joys of investing in the modern era is that much of the information you need is freely available. Indeed, London Stock Exchange rules dictate that all 'price sensitive' information (that is, information that could affect a company's share price) must be out in the open.

This information is disseminated almost exclusively through the stock exchange's own Regulatory News Service (RNS), so called because it publishes information that companies are required to make public under the exchange's regulations. This used to be the only source of announcements but in the spirit of competition other news providers are now allowed to offer alternative services. They can be identified on announcements by the three initials given for each one below in brackets.

Most companies have stuck with RNS but some use PRNewswire (PRN) and others, mainly foreign-based companies with a London listing, opt for Hugin (HUG), a European corporate communications specialist. Also authorised are Business Wire (BZW), part of Warren Buffet's Berkshire Hathaway, and Cision (CIS), an international public relations and marketing group.

Most announcements that contain new information affecting the dividend are issued at 7 am when the market is closed and appear instantaneously on those financial websites that publish regulatory news announcements, whether from RNS or a competitor. The most important ones are results announcements and possibly trading updates. We shall look at these in more detail in the next chapter.

Less price-sensitive matters, such as setting the precise sterling equivalent of a previously announced dividend denominated in a foreign currency, may be issued at any time until the RNS service closes at 6:30 pm but usually come out during the morning.

Company websites

Your primary source of information should be the company's own website. All official announcements made by the company must appear there. While a company may choose, in its statements, to highlight favourable rather than adverse happenings, it cannot pick and choose which announcements go on its website. They all go up there.

Furthermore, key figures such as sales, profits, earnings per share and dividends must be given for the past five years so you can see how the company has been progressing.

You will find recent annual reports, results announcements and trading updates in full on the website. Usually you will find them under a section labelled 'Investors' or 'Investor relations' or something similar.

If the company sells goods or services to the general public, the homepage will almost certainly be full of its products rather than financial information but a search around the site should soon reveal the right location. Try 'About us' or 'Corporate news'.

Full, fast and long-lasting information

Not only is this the fullest information you will receive but it also has the longest life. Years after you consigned your newspaper to the recycling bin the company website will still be there.

It is also a speedy source of news, as announcements go up on the website on the day they are released, and as early as possible.

Unfortunately you cannot always be sure when an announcement will be made, although results and quarterly trading updates tend to come out at much the same time each year. The Sunday and Monday editions of newspapers carry a list of company announcements due that week, although the lists will not be comprehensive.

Any announcement usually has bullet points at the front highlighting the main points of the announcement. These bullets should give you an overview of the period covered, including the key information you want – but be wary: directors, being human, may tend to accentuate or even exaggerate the positive points and play down the negative aspects.

You should go down to the income statement and look for yourself at the figures for turnover, profits, earnings per share and dividends. One column will cover the latest reporting period and there will be a second column for the corresponding period the previous year, so you can check what progress, if any, has been made.

London Stock Exchange

One of the most important changes to the London Stock Exchange website in recent years has been the introduction of comprehensive reports on each quoted company.

Look on **www.londonstockexchange.com** and click on 'Prices and Markets' and then on 'Stocks'. Alternatively, type 'Company Profiles' into the search facility. The process is a little cumbersome but you should soon get the hang of it.

You will find a five-year overview of each company's strengths, weaknesses and financial trends.

Financial websites

Possibly the best site in terms of the amount of information easily available at no cost is InvestEgate at **www.investegate.co.uk**. Log on and you go straight to the current day's UK stock market announcements. A search facility on the same page allows you to call up past announcements.

This is a particularly easy site to navigate as it is well designed and it concentrates on providing a specific range of information that is very useful for investors.

Other websites ask you to register if you want more than the brief contents of the homepage, although registration is generally free for most services. Finding your way around the sites can be daunting and the design of a site may change from time to time but take a look and see if one suits you.

Morningstar, formerly Hemscott, has the current day's announcements in full on **www.morningstar.co.uk** in the Equities section, under Regulatory News. The results for all larger and many smaller companies are interspersed with Dow Jones reports providing useful interpretation of the figures.

You will need to subscribe to Morningstar's paid-for Premium service for access to past announcements but this service does provide a good deal of other useful information, including share charts going back ten years and a comprehensive company report with figures covering turnover, profits and dividends also going back for a decade.

Other web sites with a good range of information are:

- ADVFN (**www.advfn.com**)
- MoneyAm (**www.moneyam.com**)
- Digital Look (**www.digitallook.com**).

Stockbrokers

Online and traditional stockbrokers will normally have their own websites. However you may need to have an account with them to gain access to information. Also the information available tends to vary enormously and research on individual companies normally has to be paid for.

Stockbrokers are geared up primarily to providing a share dealing service and you should pick one that provides the service you want at the best price rather than the one with the most company information freely available on its website.

However, one site worth noting is Selftrade at **www.selftrade.co.uk** which carries RNS announcements in its Market News section.

Newspapers

Even the *Financial Times (FT)* has insufficient room to carry reports on all the announcements made each day so newspapers cannot be relied upon to provide the comprehensive cover found on financial websites. In any case, the news is a day old by the time you read it while websites tell it as it happens.

Nonetheless, the *FT*, *The Times*, *The Daily Telegraph*, *The Independent* and *The Daily Mail* all provide well-written reports of major financial happenings including company results and they usually provide analysis and possibly investment advice on at least two companies.

Magazines

The two main investment magazines of interest to dividend investors are the *Investors Chronicle* and *Shares*. These are published weekly, *Shares* on Thursday and *Investors Chronicle* on Friday, and are available on newsstands or by subscription through the post.

They provide detailed analysis of selected companies and tips on shares to buy.

If you feel this would be useful, buy a copy of each and decide which you prefer. Do remember that, while both magazines try to minimise the time between writing articles and publication, there is inevitably a greater time lag than with newspapers and if you are thinking of following up a tip you should check that nothing adverse has happened at the company in the past two or three days and what the current share price is.

Summary

Our main source of information on dividends, and the first place we should look for such information, is the results announcements. The annual report is also useful, although it is on the whole mostly a confirmation of what has already been published in results for the full year. We consider what information is available and how it is presented in the next chapter.

Key points

- All price-sensitive information, including news that could affect dividends, must be released for general consumption, usually before trading starts at 7 am.

- Company news announcements may stress the good news and play down adverse factors.

Chapter 4
Results Announcements and Annual Reports

The main source of information on dividends is the results announcements that are issued, in most cases, after the half year and full year. Companies paying four dividends a year are slightly different and we will look at them separately later in the chapter.

Most results are announced between three weeks and three months after the end of the period. Larger companies tend to report more quickly because although they have more figures to add up they have greater resources to cope with the task.

In the majority of cases the announcement will start with a brief summary and/or a series of bullet points outlining the key items in the results, such as turnover and profits. Since the board will naturally want to put the most bullish items at the top of the report, we would hope to see some reference to the dividend.

As an example, the interim results for retailer Next covering the six months to the end of July 2011 and issued on 14 September began thus:

Results for the Half Year Ended July 2011

In a difficult year Next has proven resilient. Group revenue for the first half was 3.6% higher than last year and profit before tax was up 8.5% on a continuing basis. The business remains strongly cash generative and continued buyback of shares further enhanced growth in earnings per share, which were 18.6% ahead of last year. The interim dividend increases by 10% to 27.5p per share. Financial highlights from our continuing business are as follows:

- revenue up 3.6% to £1,565m

- profit before tax up 8.5% to £228m

- earnings per share up 18.6% to 98.3p

- net debt of £640m and committed facilities of £918m

- interim dividend up 10% to 27.5p per share.

We should be suspicious but not paranoid if there is no mention of the dividend in the bullet points, or if the company launches straight into its report without picking out the salient facts. It could mean that there is no dividend or that the dividend has been held at a low level. However, it has to be said that some companies inexplicably hide their light under a bushel, so in such cases we will need to check further down the announcement to ascertain what the situation is regarding the dividend.

Back to the Next announcement.

The interim dividend has been raised by 10%, which is obviously great news. Companies tend to be cautious at half year, especially if their business is in any way seasonal. Although Next, selling fashions and homewares, is not as dependent on Christmas as some retailers, it still sells more goods in its second half to the end of January.

Furthermore, retailing was at the time suffering from rising costs and falling consumer confience so a 10% increase in the interim dividend was a real vote of confidence in itself. We can see from the bullet points that earnings per share were actually up by more than the dividend, so the dividend increase looks well justified and sustainable.

The final dividend, which as we noted in an earlier chapter is almost always larger than the interim and is often twice as large, may not be increased by the same percentage. Nonetheless, we can normally work on the basis that it will be, barring unforeseen circumstances.

By the time that the interim results are out any company will already have seen the first few weeks of second half trading and may, depending on the line of business it is in, have a good idea of how orders are flowing in.

One other point mentioned earlier also applies here: if the company is rebalancing its dividends to achieve a different proportion between the interim and the final, then we must tailor our expectations for the final dividend accordingly.

We should look for further clues in what the key executives say in the announcement. Usually the chairperson, the chief executive, the finance director or any combination of the three will have their say.

Sure enough, in the Next announcement we find a heading that says:

Chief Executive's Review

Headlines

- Sales up 3.6%
- Profit up 8.5%
- Earnings per share up 18.6%
- Dividend up 2.5p to 27.5p

We have the original bullet points rehashed, this time with figures rather than percentages. So we now know the actual level of the dividend in pence and the increase in pence.

Further clues as to how the company is progressing, and thus the prospects for the final dividend, will be found in this review. So, again, reproducing from the Next announcement, we see:

Overview

Looking ahead to our full-year results, we believe that sales for the year will be between 2.0% and 4.5% ahead of last year, which would result in Group profits being up between +0.4% and +8.7% and EPS [Earnings Per Share] up between +7.5% and +16.4%.

Early indications are that retail headwinds are likely to ease as we move into 2012. We have strong evidence that there will be little or no inflation in our own prices and it seems probable that other inflationary pressures will ease as commodity price rises begin to annualise in the first quarter of 2012.

The overview may contain specific projected figures for the next quarter or, at the other extreme, a few meaningless platitudes. It may, as in this case, contain figures and a brief description of how events are unfolding. In any event the overview is quite likely to be short and we should not worry if it is brief provided it does actually tell us something.

Larger companies, especially those with international operations, may go into greater detail of how things are panning out in different parts of the business. There may also be greater detail if something momentous has happened, such as the scrapping of the dividend or the takeover of another company.

How useful any figures are depends on the company's visibility of earnings. In the case of Next, it cannot reasonably see too far ahead as sales rely on the public mood and costs are at the mercy of volatile prices of energy and raw materials. Thus we have a wide spread in the forecasts for sales and profits.

The key part of the Next overview is that inflation, which had been running well above the Bank of England target of 2% for more than two years and was around 5% at the time of the statement, was easing off. Thus Next would have one less problem to cope with and would not be faced with trying to pass rising prices onto its customers.

Way, way down the statement, usually well after a series of tables showing the results and other figures, you will find something like this:

Dividend

The interim dividend is being increased by 2.5p to 27.5p. This will be paid on 3 January 2012 to shareholders on the register at 25 November 2011. The shares will trade ex-dividend from 23 November. For the full year we intend to raise the total of dividends payable by a similar percentage to the growth in basic earnings per share from continuing business.

This, as we can see, gives details of the size of the dividend, when it goes ex-dividend and when it will be paid.

In this case, although it does not always happen, we have the bonus of a clear indication of intent regarding the final dividend. Note that Next is clearly expecting to raise the final dividend, although not necessarily by the same percentage as it raised the interim dividend. Much will depend on where earnings per share come in within the 7.5% to 16.4% range indicated in the overview.

Within the tables contained in the announcement you will see one that tells you how much the dividend is costing the company:

Statement of changes in total equity			
	Six months to July 2011 (£m)	Six months to July 2010 (£m)	Year to January 2011 (£m)
Equity dividends paid	(89.5)	(85.4)	(129.6)

This simply records how much money the company paid out in dividends in the current period, in the comparable period of the previous year, and in the previous year as a whole. The figure appears in brackets because it is a payment made by the company rather than money received, just as, for example, interest payments made by the company are shown in brackets.

This figure will probably be of little interest to you. After all, your main concern is how much dividend per share you are getting. However, the figure can be useful to compare against profits and cash flow so you can be satisfied that the company can afford the dividend.

It is also useful if the company has issued shares in an acquisition, rights issue or placing. You can see if the total amount of the dividend has increased or whether the same amount of cash is being spread more thinly.

Note that, although Next's final dividend is greater than its interim, it paid out more in dividends in the first half than in the second. This is quite normal. The paradox arises because the (smaller) interim dividend is paid out in the second half of the year while the (larger) final dividend falls into the following first half.

A company may feel moved to spell this out to readers, unfortunately not always in easy-to-understand terms, as this paragraph from the GlaxoSmithKline 2010 annual report demonstrates:

> Under IFRS interim dividends are only recognised in the financial statements when paid and not when declared. GSK normally pays a dividend two quarters after the quarter to which it relates and one quarter after it is declared. The 2010 financial statements recognise those dividends paid in 2010, namely the third and fourth interim dividends for 2009 and the first and second interim dividends for 2010.

All Glaxo is saying is that its first two quarterly dividends appear in the accounts for the years in which they are declared, because they are paid before the financial year end, while dividends for the third and fourth quarters are paid after the year end and are therefore included in the following year's accounts. Thus the accounts for 2010 show the amounts paid for the last two dividends of 2009 and only the first two for 2010. The two later 2010 dividends will be counted in the 2011 accounts.

On the whole, the annual report will tell you very little about the dividend that was not included in the results announcement. The exception is that the annual report will include a five-year record of dividend payments, something you rarely get in with the results. Thus DIY group Kingfisher included this table in its 2011 annual report:

Group five year financial summary

Financial year	2006-7	2007-8	2008-9	2009-10	2010-11
Basic earnings per share	13.6p	10.9p	0.2p	16.5p	21.0p
Adjusted basic earnings per share	10.6p	10.6p	11p	16.4p	20.5p
Dividend per share	10.65p	7.25p	5.325p	5.5p	7.07p

We can see that Kingfisher was transformed from a group struggling to cover its dividend even once to one with a progressive dividend policy and cover of nearly three times. This was achieved by reducing the dividend to a sustainable level and through a re-organisation in 2008-9 when asset writedowns almost wiped out earnings per share.

Note the importance of adjusted earnings per share in this table as this figure shows underlying earnings before exceptional items and gives a clearer picture of progress over the five years.

It would be useful if all annual reports contained this five-year table in exactly the same place and in exactly the same format. This does not happen. Some companies put the table proudly near the front while others bury it. Sometimes it appears as a table and sometimes as a bar chart.

It is much easier to search for the figures if you have the annual report in paper form. If you are looking online it may be a case of wading through the annual report page by page until you unearth it.

Key points

- The interim and full-year results announcements tell you how much the latest dividend is and by how much it has been increased or decreased.

- Look through the results for any clue as to what the next dividend is likely to be.

- You may have to search through the annual report for the vital five-year dividend record but it is worth the effort for the fuller picture it gives.

Chapter 5
Tax

It's great to be earning a return on your careful investment but, alas, the Chancellor of the Exchequer wants his cut. There are three main taxes that are likely to affect dividend investors:

1. stamp duty
2. income tax
3. capital gains tax.

We will look at each in turn below.

1. Stamp duty

For a start, we are stuck with the 0.5% stamp duty on share purchases. Various campaigns to have this impost scrapped, most notable at one stage by the London Stock Exchange, have prompted not a glimmer of interest from successive Chancellors of the Exchequer.

Nor has the emergence of financial spread betting or contracts for difference, which avoid stamp duty, forced any official rethink.

It is just too easy a tax to collect and is impossible for share buyers to avoid so why should the Government give up a handy source of revenue? Perhaps we should be grateful that there has not been any increase in the duty, as has happened with stamp duty for house purchases.

One thing that dividend investors can do is to buy for the long term and reduce the number of purchases they make. This is good discipline, for dividend investors should be looking to retain their portfolios for years rather than months or weeks anyway.

Since stamp duty is a percentage rather than a flat rate per transaction, it does not matter whether we buy shares in one batch or in several tranches.

This is important for new investors with a comparatively small sum who are seeking to build a balanced portfolio from scratch. You can spread your investments across several companies and sectors while retaining the option of topping up each holding when funds are more plentiful.

2. Income tax

Most investors, including those drawing pensions, will be paying income tax. For details of the latest allowances and tax rates for income from jobs, pensions and savings accounts, visit: **www.hmrc.gov.uk/rates/it.htm**

This site is actually quite clear and well set out.

Personal allowances

For the tax year 2011-12 the personal allowances (i.e. the income that can be earned that is not taxed) are:

Table 5.1 – UK tax allowances 2011–12

Age	Allowance
Under 65	£7,475
65-74	£9,940
75 and over	£10,090

In defiance of HM Revenue & Customs' advertisements claiming that tax does not have to be taxing, matters are further complicated because allowances are withdrawn at the rate of £1 for every extra £2 earned above certain levels.

Those aged 65 and over start to lose their extra entitlement if they earn more than £24,000 in any tax year. So those aged 65-74 get only the basic personal allowance if their income is more than £26,465; for those aged 75 and over the figure is £26,615.

Furthermore, the personal allowance is gradually withdrawn, again at the rate of £1 for every £2 of extra income over £100,000. So everyone earning £114,950 or more, irrespective of their age, lost their entire personal allowance for 2011-12.

Remember that personal allowances tend to go up year by year so it is worth checking the official HMRC site for changes.

Income tax rates

Income tax rates are shown in the following table.

Table 5.2 – UK income tax rates 2011-12

Taxable earnings	Tax rate
Up to £35,000	20%
£35,001–£150,000	40%
Over £150,000	50%

Taxable earnings are earnings net of personal allowances.

Tax on dividends

Just to make the whole process a little more taxing, income from company shares, unit trusts and open-ended investment companies (OEICs) is taxed at different rates to income from jobs and pensions. Details are to be found at:

www.direct.gov.uk/en/MoneyTaxAndBenefits/Taxes/TaxOnSavings AndInvestments/DG_4016453

For 2011-12 the tax rates are shown in Table 5.3.

Table 5.3 – UK income tax rates on dividends 2011–12

Dividend income	Tax rate	Rate after tax credit
Below £35,000	10%	0%
£35,000–£150,000	32.5%	25%
Above £150,000	42.5%	36.1%

The 10% tax is deemed to have been paid by the company out of its profits, so the dividend is paid to you net of the 10%. The tax man 'credits' you with having already paid 10% tax before you receive the dividend.

So the actual rate you pay when you declare the dividends on your income tax form are less than the tax rate. If you do not pay income tax, however, you cannot recover the 10% paid by the company because it is deemed to be a tax credit!

If you can make sense of all that, don't apply for a job with the Treasury. Tax rules are laid down by the Chancellor of the Exchequer in his Budget and Chancellors do not understand simplicity.

You will receive a voucher with any dividends you receive, either on paper or electronically, stating the amount of dividend paid to you and the amount of tax credit. Include the figures on your annual income tax form.

3. Capital gains tax

Do not assume because you are investing primarily for dividends rather than making a quick buck that you need not bother about capital gains tax. Although it is a much less pressing matter than income tax, you should be aware of how the tax is calculated and how to minimise your potential exposure to it.

Profit on buying and selling shares is subject to capital gains tax, set at 28% (18% for lower-rate taxpayers) of the gain in the 2011-12 tax year and subject to revision in the Chancellor's annual budget.

Details can be found on the website: **www.hmrc.gov.uk/rates/cgt.htm**

You also get an allowance in the same way that you receive a personal income tax allowance before the tax rate kicks in. For 2011-12 the allowance was set at £10,600.

Clearly, the greater the size of your investments the greater the chance that you will incur capital gains tax should you decide to sell. Also, if you have investments outside shares, such as in property, you are at greater risk.

In March every year, just before the financial year ends, it is worth considering whether to realise any capital gains, taking care to stay within the allowance or not to stray too far above it. If you have already incurred a large capital gain during the course of the financial year, decide whether to sell any loss makers among your share portfolio to offset against the gain.

ISAs

You can reduce your exposure to income tax and capital gains tax by buying shares through an Individual Savings Account (ISA). There is, unfortunately, a limit to how much you can invest in an ISA each tax year. The figure is £10,680 for 2011-12, increasing roughly in line with the Retail Price Index (RPI) for subsequent years.

The HRMC website has a different page for different tax years, so the simplest option for finding the allowance in subsequent years will be to type 'Individual Savings Accounts' into your computer search engine. There will be no shortage of personal finance websites willing to supply the figure.

All dividend income from shares held in an ISA, and all capital gains made from selling them, is tax free. The higher the tax bracket you are in, the greater the income tax benefit.

You cannot, however, claim back the 10% tax credit that we noted in the section on income tax earlier in this chapter.

Putting core holdings into your ISA

The main question is whether you should put your core holdings, the ones you see as the longest term investments, into the ISA or the ones you are most likely to part with if the price is right.

Since dividends are repeated every year, as a general rule it makes most sense to put your core holdings into your ISA. Once an ISA investment has been sold it cannot be replaced. The capital gains tax saving is purely one off.

While it is always tempting to beat the tax man, we should not allow this pleasure to distort our investments. Do not rush to use up your entitlement if you cannot identify an attractive purchase. Nor should you baulk at selling a doubtful company in your ISA entitlement just because it cannot be replaced. Losses from hasty or ill judged decisions will far outweigh your tax gains.

One final point is that AIM stocks cannot be put into ISAs. Do not lose too much sleep over that. AIM stocks offer far fewer prospects for dividend investors than the main stock exchange listings.

AIM-quoted companies are more likely to pay no dividend or to scrap an existing dividend. They are also less likely to have a progressive dividend policy.

Key points

- Do not let tax considerations override your investment decisions.
- Use your ISA allowance in full if you can.
- Put your core long-term holdings into ISAs.
- Review your portfolio towards the end of each tax year.

Chapter 6
A Year in the Life of a
Dividend Paying Company

Now that we have set out the basics, we can see how they apply to companies by looking at a dividend paying company over the course of 12 months.

FirstGroup runs buses and trains in the UK and also has operations in the United States, where it owns the famous Greyhound coaches and also operates services such as school buses under contract. Its financial year runs from 1 April to 31 March.

To put the situation in context, FirstGroup had issued its full-year results for 2008-9 on 13 May 2009. It had declared a final dividend of 12.7p, making a total of 18.75p for the year.

The final dividend was paid on 21 August 2009 to shareholders on the register on 17 July 2009. It cost £61.1 million, easily covered by inward cash flow that year of £639.7 million.

FirstGroup paid an interim dividend of 6.65p on 3 February 2010, an increase of 10% (over the interim dividend paid the previous year), for the first half of the 2009-10 financial year.

2010

31 March

We take up its story at the start of its 2010-11 financial year with the issuing of a trading update. Inevitably, the start of the financial year for any company tends to dominated by what has happened over the previous 12 months but we need to start in this rather back-to-front way because the announcements covering the past year set the scene for the new one.

The trading update began with a summary in the form of bullet points:

SUMMARY

- Overall performance is in line with management's expectations.

- Group on course to deliver earnings and cash targets for the year including £100 million cash generation to reduce net debt.

- Achieved cost reductions of over £200 million per annum – mitigating effect of recession on trading and increased hedged fuel costs this year.

We can see for a start that no nasty surprises have cropped up since the previous trading statement at the end of FirstGroup's third quarter. On the contrary, the transport operator is generating cash which will cut debt and thus reduce the interest bill, leaving more cash available to meet future dividends.

Although FirstGroup has been affected by the double squeeze of reduced income and rising fuel costs, it has taken action to curb the impact.

However, because we are always alert to a possible sting in the tail, we read through the statement just to be sure that management is not putting the best gloss on the situation.

Under the heading 'Overall trading' we note that specific figures are given: "Severe weather in the previous winter cost £16 million in lost operating profit and the fuel bill went up by £100 million. These were more than offset by savings of £200 million."

We are also naturally interested in how the new financial year is likely to pan out so we find:

OUTLOOK

The global economic outlook remains uncertain and in particular we expect to see continued pressure on public spending budgets in North America. Against this backdrop we expect moderate earnings growth. Net debt reduction remains a key priority and we are confident in our ability to deliver our cash target of at least £100 million in 2010-11 to reduce net debt and to develop further opportunities to increase cash generation within the Group to accelerate our deleveraging plans.

Despite the cautious note we are pleased that the company is alive to the challenges and taking appropriate action. In particular we are reassured that reducing the debt burden is being speeded up. Net debt had been as high as £2.5 billion and was still well over £2 billion.

This reassurance failed to save the shares from falling 15p to 359p on the day of the announcement. That did provide any interested investors with a potential buying opportunity.

Early April

The new financial year got off to an uncertain start with the Rail, Maritime & Transport (RMT) union threatening a nationwide four-day strike affecting all rail companies over Easter.

It was delayed when National Rail, the network operator, obtained a court injunction alleging discrepancies in RMT's strike ballot but RMT also called, separately, a strike in FirstGroup's First Scotrail operations on 12 April.

Both strikes were averted but were a distraction for management, especially as FirstGroup was at the time considering possible offers for its GB Railfreight business.

12 May

Results for the year that had ended on 31 March were issued. They showed:

FirstGroup	2008-9	2009-10	Change
Revenue	£6,187.3 million	£6,319.0 million	+ 2.1%
Pre-tax profits	£200.0 million	£173.3 million	- 10.2%
Earnings per share	30.2p	26.9p	- 8.9%
Total dividend	18.75p	20.65p	+ 10.1%

FirstGroup gave a detailed breakdown of its various operations, splitting rail from bus and UK from the US. It also highlighted the issues it faced, such as falling passenger numbers and rising fuel costs, and the actions it was taking to offset the impact.

Dividend investors would be pleased to see the increase in the dividend but wary that the statement showed dividend cover falling further, from 1.6 to only 1.3.

The announcement indicated that the final dividend would be paid on 20 August to shareholders on the register on 16 July.

1 June

GB Railfreight is sold to Eurotunnel for £31 million as FirstGroup reiterates its intention to focus on core businesses in the UK and US. Proceeds are to be used to reduce debt. Although it is a drop in the ocean of more than £2 billion debt, this is reassuring given the danger that the debt burden could threaten the dividend.

FirstGroup reiterated its intention to generate £150 million net cash in the current financial year.

8 July

A first quarter trading statement is issued at the AGM.

Highlights show:

- current trading in line with management expectations

- continued focus on priorities of cost control, managing the network to protect margins, increased cash generation and net debt reduction

- expecting to achieve moderate earnings growth during the first half

The implication is that progress is being made, albeit not spectacularly, that management is keeping its eye on key issues and the dividend will be at least maintained unless unforeseen disaster strikes.

22 September

Chief Executive Sir Moir Lockhead announces that he will retire after 21 years in the post. His deputy Tim O'Toole, who has been on the board for two years, is to succeed him. While it is always disconcerting when a long-standing chief executive quits, this is an orderly succession and not the result of a falling out. There will be a five-month overlap between O'Toole taking the reins and Lockhead actually retiring.

29 September

A trading update covering the first half effectively repeats the AGM statement and in particular stresses strong cash generation. It says that first-half results will be issued on 3 November.

3 November

Highlights of the half-year results statement are:

PERFORMANCE IN LINE WITH EXPECTATIONS WITH STRONG CASH PERFORMANCE IN THE PERIOD

- total Group revenue up by 4.0% including improving rail volumes

- adjusted basic EPS up 16.7% – on track to deliver moderate earnings growth for the full year

- strong cash performance expected to continue – target for full-year net cash generation increased from £150 million to £180 million (excluding business disposal proceeds)

- interim dividend increased by 7.1% to 7.12p.

The last line is the one we want to see first – and it makes great reading. This increase was way ahead of inflation, running at about 4% at the time. We can feel confident that the final dividend is likely to rise by a similar amount, for although revenue has grown more slowly, earnings have zoomed.

Equally encouraging is that debt is being cleared faster than expected, even without counting in the proceeds of the sale of GB Railfreight.

The statement details progress in each part of the operation and there appear to be no specific areas of serious concern:

First Student, the US school bus operation, was the weakest part, with revenue down 0.9% as school budgets were squeezed but this had been offset by cost reductions.

First Transit, US bus services, grew revenue by 5.5% and Greyhound, the long-distance coach service, attracted more passengers.

UK Bus passenger revenue was up, with the improvement accelerating in the second quarter, while cost controls improved margins. There is capacity to increase the network as passenger numbers increase.

UK Rail passenger numbers were up strongly.

Figures in the financial summary confirmed the progress, as we see in the following table.

FirstGroup	2009–10	2010–11	Change (%)
Revenue (£m)	2,958.2	3,075.8	+4.0
Pre-tax profit (£m)	28.6	82.0	+186.7
Adjusted profit (£m)	68.0	77.7	+14.3
Basic EPS (p)	3.6	11.4	+216.7
Adjusted EPS (p)	9.0	10.5	+16.7
Interim dividend (p)	6.65	7.12	+7.1
Net debt (£m)	2,373.8	2,190.8	-7.7

The adjusted profit and EPS figures strip out exceptional items to give a truer reflection of the underlying rate of improvement.

It is always worth looking down the statement to see if there is any specific reference to the dividend, particularly at the half-year stage when there may be an indication of the likely level of the full-year payout. In this case, among comments by the new Chief Executive Tim O'Toole, we find this paragraph:

> This strong performance, particularly against the challenging economic backdrop, demonstrates the highly cash generative nature of the Group. This together with the expectation of moderate earnings growth in the full year enables the Group to increase capital expenditure and supports the Board's policy to increase dividends by at least 7% per annum as well as deliver a reduction in net debt.

So there we have it. There is enough cash being generated to develop the business, reduce debt and still pay a 7% increase in the dividend.

One further point is that O'Toole is continuing existing policies that seem to be working rather than waving a new broom for the sake of stamping his own name on the company.

The interim dividend was paid on 3 February 2011 to shareholders on the register on 8 January. It came out of an inward cash flow of £164.4 million.

13 December

Important new banking facilities are arranged:

> FirstGroup announces that it has recently signed $1,400 million of five-year committed bank facilities to refinance $1,500 million of existing revolving bank facilities that were due to mature in February 2012.

This is good news for dividend investors on several levels.

1. The new facilities are for *less* than the existing facilities. While that would be bad news if the company needed money to expand or to stay in business, this is a reflection of the way in which FirstGroup is reducing its borrowings in line with its stated policy.

2. Banks are committed to lending for a fixed term rather than having the option under the existing revolving facilities to call in the loan.

3. The loan has been re-negotiated well ahead of the expiry date of the existing facilities. This means that management would not be distracted over the following months by desperate attempts to get new facilities in place before the old ones ran out.

4. Facilities agreed well in advance tend to be at better rates of interest and on less onerous terms. Clearly, the banks have not been digging their heels in and are apparently relaxed about continuing to lend.

5. An early agreement indicates that FirstGroup management is on top of its game with forward-looking startegies.

6. Because the Group has operations in the US, with revenue and spending in dollars, it makes sense to have some of its loan facilities in the US currency.

2011

13 January

A routine quarterly trading update is issued starting with these bullet points:

**FIRSTGROUP PLC
INTERIM MANAGEMENT STATEMENT**

FirstGroup provides the following update on trading during the third quarter from 1 October to 31 December 2010.

Summary

- overall trading in line with management expectations
- remain on course to achieve earnings and cash targets for the year
- confident of achieving Group's target of 2.5x net debt: EBITDA by March 2011
- Continued proactive management of debt – $1.4bn of new five-year committed bank facilities signed to replace debt due to mature in February 2012.

We quickly get the message that there is really nothing much new in this update, although that is no bad thing because it means nothing nasty has cropped up to take the Group off course. There is, however, a comment on the severe winter weather that disrupted transport that Christmas:

> The Group provided an update on trading as part of its half-yearly financial results announcement on 3 November 2010. Since then, the trading environment has remained challenging. The prolonged and widespread disruption, particularly in the UK, caused by severe weather during the period impacted UK Bus and Rail profits by around GBP7m. However, the Group remains on course to achieve its earnings and cash targets for the year.

> The inherent strength of the Group is demonstrated by the continued strong cash generation. Initiatives to increase cash generation within the Group and to deliver improvements in working capital continue to produce encouraging results. We remain confident of achieving our target ratio of 2.5x net debt:EBITDA by March 2011.

FirstGroup has put a figure on the lost profits, which is helpful and suggests that the company is being upfront with bad news. It also implies that management has control of the business, so it has been able to assess the damage quickly.

Bad weather in winter is an occupational hazard for a transport company and we would have expected FirtstGroup to have made some allowance for this happening in its earlier pronouncement. We are reassured that indeed the company is still in line to meet its earlier stated targets.

Always look for an outlook statement lower down the announcement. This one by FirstGroup was rounded off by:

OUTLOOK

Overall trading remains in line with management's expectations. Our drive to increase cash generation within the Group is delivering results and, as previously reported, we continue to expect moderate earnings growth in the current financial year. This, together with the Board's confidence in the Group's ability to continue to deliver long-term value for shareholders, supports the commitment to grow dividends by at least 7% per annum.

---

11 March

A further trading update precedes year end – it has appeared earlier than the one to mark the end of the previous financial year, so we should look carefully if there is any obvious reason.

SUMMARY

- The Group remains on course to achieve overall earnings and cash targets for the year and 2.5x net debt:EBITDA at March 2011.

- Outperformance in UK operations, particularly Rail division, offset by further pressure on First Student's margin.

No worries, it seems that everything is still on target, with difficulties in the US school bus operation offset by progress in other parts of the Group. Indeed, the statement goes on to say as much:

> The strength of the Group is underpinned by the diversity of its portfolio with separate areas of the business moving through the economic cycle at different times. We remain encouraged by improving trends in some of our markets, however the trading environment for First Student remains challenging.
>
> The highly cash generative nature of the Group, together with the expectation of moderate earnings growth this financial year supports the Board's policy to increase dividends by at least 7% per annum alongside our net debt reduction programme.

The reassurance on the level of dividend and the reduction of debt is there again.

And so the year has come full circle, ending and beginning with a summary of the past 12 months and the outlook for the financial year just beginning.

Key points

Routine announcements such as results and trading statements come out at regular intervals.

- Check whether the overall message has changed.

- Always read any outlook statement.

- Check for any specific references to the dividend.

PART B

Dividend Analysis

Chapter 7
Profits, Dividends and Cash Flow

You don't need complicated mathematical calculations or fancy trading systems to begin to invest for dividends. Basic analysis is not rocket science. The most important figures are quite simple and blindingly obvious. Start by asking three basic questions:

1. Does a company have a track record of producing steadily rising profits?

2. Does it have a track record of steadily rising dividends?

3. Does it generate cash to pay those dividends?

In this chapter we will look at these three questions in turn.

1. Profits

In the end, dividends are paid out of profits. If a company is not making a profit it is unlikely to pay a dividend and even if it does the pleasure will be short-lived. While a company can stand the odd downward blip in profits, it cannot survive for long on thin air.

Companies publish a five-year track record in their annual reports and that is a sensible time to trace back. Beyond that, so much could have changed as to make comparisons fairly meaningless, even if you can find data far enough back.

Bear in mind that the past will not necessarily be repeated this year or next, and will almost certainly not be repeated exactly. However, the performance of the company in producing profits in recent years is your best guide to how it is likely to perform in the immediate future.

Let us look at the five-year track record for profits from four companies in different parts of the retail sector:

Table 7.1– Profit history for four sample retail companies

Company	2006–07 (£m)	2007–08 (£m)	2008–09 (£m)	2009–10 (£m)	2010–11 (£m)
Kingfisher	406	391	387	569	698
Tesco	2,424	2,793	2,619	2,942	3,182
Mothercare	21	41	48	33	13
Debenhams	128	103	121	146	160

Source: Morningstar Premium

For this illustration we have use normalised profits, that is profits that have had exceptional items stripped out. By removing large items that will not be repeated in other years we can see the genuine underlying movement in profits. Pre-tax profits will tend to fluctuate more, although it is perfectly reasonable to use the pre-tax figure if you prefer.

We can see that every company has had at least one dip in profits but we can also see that the underlying trends do differ. Yet all were affected by similar factors such as the restraints on consumer spending coupled with rising costs.

Most retailers employ large numbers of staff on the minimum wage, which has continued to rise. Soaring fuel costs make distributing goods to the stores more expensive and adds to electricity bills. Inflation has boosted the prices of raw materials and finished goods.

Looking briefly at each company:

- **Kingfisher:** The owner of DIY chain B&Q struggled in the aftermath of the credit crunch but has bounced back strongly. Perhaps people who put off home improvements until they saw how badly they were affected by the global downturn finally decided to go ahead anyway. Those who hoped to move house but could not raise a mortgage may have opted to make the most of the homes they already had. In any event, profits have bounced back well past their previous peak.

- **Tesco:** The UK's largest supermarket has expanded successfully in Europe as well but it still managed a hiccup in 2008-9. This was not a particularly serious dip – profits were still higher than they were two years earlier and they soon resumed their upward march. Supermarkets are more sheltered from the economic downturn than most retailers because we still have to eat but Tesco's push into non-food items made it potentially vulnerable to reduced consumer spending. Also supermarkets are notorious for bouts of price wars, often instigated by Tesco. Nor are they safe from the pressures of rising costs.

- **Mothercare:** It was all going so well until the middle of the period before profits tailed off in an alarming fashion. It is not readily obvious why a management team that had worked wonders over several years suddenly lost its touch but all the pressures on retailers have been felt keenly.

- **Debenhams:** The department store gained notoriety as one of the worst stock market flotations for investors to get involved in. Having been bought out by venture capitalists, it was re-floated in 2006 loaded with too much debt and the shares bombed for two years. However, profits have recovered and the upward path has been sufficiently well established to suggest that the shares might now be worth looking at.

2. Dividends

Having established whether a company is making profits, and whether those profits are growing, we can turn to the dividend.

Again, we can take the four retail companies whose profits we looked at:

Table 7.2 – Dividend history for four sample retail companies

Company	2006–07	2007–08	2008–09	2009–10	2010–11
Kingfisher	10.65p	7.25p	5.32p	5.5p	7.07p
Tesco	9.64p	10.9p	11.96p	13.05p	14.06p
Mothercare	10.0p	12.0p	14.5p	16.8p	18.3p
Debenhams	6.28p	3p	0p	0p	3p

Source: London Stock Exchange

Some comments on each company:

- **Kingfisher:** Those concerns about Kingfisher profits are reflected in the dividend, which had halved by 2008-9. However, let us not judge in haste. Kingfisher's dividend has started to rise again. It is clear that the Kingfisher board sensibly accepted that a dividend of more than 10p was no longer sustainable given the fall in profits and so the dividend was rebased at a lower, viable level.

- **Tesco:** Here we see a steadily rising dividend to match the steadily rising profits. This is the kind of investment we are looking for.

- **Mothercare:** On the surface this looks to be an equally attractive investment to rank alongside Tesco but the drastic slump in profits alerts us to the fact that the dividend rises are not sustainable unless there is a dramatic improvement in the company's performance.

- **Debenhams:** This has been a roller-coaster rise with the dividend rising and falling, then disappearing and finally being re-instated.

This is not a great track record and we are hardly assured that dividends are here to stay, let alone rise over the years. The dividend table is far less reassuring than that for profits.

By reading the two tables together we have identified Tesco as having the best record overall; Kingfisher represents a potential recovery stock; Debenhams is very risky; and Mothercare is one to avoid.

We shall look in closer detail at progressive dividends in the next chapter.

3. Cash flow

Our table below shows the amount of cash that flowed into the company each year expressed as the amount received for each share in issue. This calculation gives us a better comparison of how well each company is doing than presenting the total inflow, as it gives us an equivalent figure irrespective of the size of the company.

Table 7.3 – Cash flow history for four sample retail companies

Company	2006–07	2007–08	2008–09	2009–10	2010–11
Kingfisher	21.3p	16.4p	53.1p	45.6p	26.3p
Tesco	35.5p	45.2p	51.6p	61.3p	52.1p
Mothercare	39.5p	64.9p	41.8p	58.8p	31.0p
Debenhams	32.3p	26.8p	22.2p	16.7p	16.1p

Source: Morningstar Premium

We can see that despite the varied performances of the companies we selected they have one thing in common as far as cash flow is concerned: the amount swings around considerably. This is not a big worry.

Cash flow will vary from year to year as the company faces varying calls on its resources. Capital spending in particular can mop up cash and retailers are forever finding new premises, closing and selling underperforming stores and refurbishing tired-looking outlets.

What is important is that over the years cash has come in rather than out and that sufficient cash has been generated to pay the dividend. We will look at cash flow in greater detail in chapter 9.

Note: Remember that this summary is based purely on our initial reactions to a set of figures at one moment in time. Things can go wrong subsequently and problems can be addressed in the future.

The figures should also be read in the context of the economic environment in which these companies operated.

We have already remarked on the fact that the retail sector generally faced considerable difficulties such as rising costs, most of which were difficult to avoid. Questions we should be asking of the four companies we selected are:

1. Do people need to buy the goods they sell?

2. Do they own their own stores or are they at the mercy of landlords that may raise rents?

3. Are their internal costs under control?

4. How well are their distribution systems working?

5. Do they update products to match changing needs or fashions?

6. Are they dependent on the UK economy or do they have outlets overseas?

You will obviously need to adapt these questions to suit the company you are analysing but the issues to investigate at this stage are basic ones about the general health of:

1. the **country** or countries in which the company operates

2. the **sector** it is in

3. the **sub-sector** it is in.

This is known as *bottom-up investing*, where you start with an attractive-looking company and work your way up to the wider world in which it operates.

You can do this exercise the other way round by identifying promising countries to invest in and working your way down to find the best sectors, the best sub-sectors and the best companies within them. This is known as *top-down investing*.

Either method is perfectly legitimate and even among professionals views differ on which is the better method. The answer is to try both and find which suits you.

Key points

- Profits, dividends and cash flow are your first considerations in selecting a possible investment.

- These are basic, uncomplicated figures that do not need a qualification in mathematics.

- Look back over a five-year period to see the trends rather than relying on the latest figures alone.

Chapter 8
Progressive Dividends

Now this does matter, and it matters very much. We want companies with what is known as a *progressive dividend policy*, that is the dividend is increased year by year. This means that our income will rise to offset inflation.

You need to check back over the past five years to see whether a company has been increasing its profits, its earnings per share and its dividends. Generally speaking, these three figures will go hand in hand over time. Higher profits translate into higher earnings per share – as the larger cake divides into larger slices, and as earnings per share rise, the scope for raising the dividend increases correspondingly.

This will not be an exact correlation. Profits do not rise in a steady line, while the dividend will rise more smoothly. Directors will tend to even out the upward trend when declaring the dividend to avoid disappointing shareholders in the years when profits rise by very little. This smoothing out also allows for an increased dividend even if profits dip temporarily.

Past success is not a guarantee for the future and we should always consider what might happen next. The good times may be coming to an end; conversely, a poorly performing company may be turning the corner.

We should also remember that companies with progressive dividend policies will be attractive to all dividend investors. The shares may be relatively expensive, reflecting the hopes for continued success.

Checking the history of dividends

The first place to look for a history of dividend payments is the website of the company itself. For example, to find the dividend history of Next Plc, go to the Next website (**www.nextplc.co.uk**), select 'Investors' from the menu and then 'Dividend history'. The dividend information can usually be found in a similar location for most companies.

A shortcut can be to search on Google with a phrase like, 'dividend history of Next Plc'.

Alternatively the London Stock Exchange website has data for all quoted companies at

www.londonstockexchange.com/exchange/prices-and-markets/stock s/prices-search/stock-prices-search.html

Or you can go to an online data service such as:

- **www.northcote.co.uk**

- **www.morningstar.co.uk**

Software programs such as Sharescope also have dividend histories. So, fortunately, it is not usually a problem finding this information.

A sample of some FTSE 350 companies and their dividends paid for the past 9 years is given in the following table.

Table 8.1 – Dividend histories for a selection of FTSE 100 companies

Company	Dividend (8 years ago)	Dividend (7 years ago)	Dividend (6 years ago)	Dividend (5 years ago)	Dividend (4 years ago)	Dividend (3 years ago)	Dividend (2 years ago)	Dividend (1 year ago)	Dividend (most recent)
Aegis Group	1.25	1.32	1.46	1.65	1.9	2.3	2.5	2.5	2.75
Aggreko	5.73	5.83	6.01	6.31	6.94	8.32	10.41	13.01	19.51
AMEC	10	10.5	11	11.5	12.2	13.4	15.4	17.7	26.5
Amlin	1.96	2.45	7.84	10.64	12.51	15	17	20	23
Anglo American	33.19	31.71	37.93	57.66	58	61.92	23.86	0	40.48
Antofagasta	3.48	3.95	4.14	4.29	4.2	4.34	5.55	6.1	10.23
Associated British Foods	13.25	14.6	16.4	18	18.75	19.5	20.25	21	23.8
AstraZeneca	43	40.9	50.3	73.7	89.6	93	132.6	141.4	161.6
Aviva	23	24.15	25.36	27.27	30	33	33	24	25.5
Carnival	26.23	25.58	27.49	44.39	54.75	68.47	89.59	0	26.52
Carpetright	37	44	47	49	50	52	8	16	8
Centrica	3.54	4.78	7.66	9.35	9.93	11.57	12.63	12.8	14.3
Glaxo SmithKline	40	41	42	44	48	53	57	61	65
John Wood Group	2.39	2.38	2.39	3	3.33	4.5	7.27	8.28	9.07
Land Securities Group	31.55	32.97	38.43	41.5	47.1	56.87	51.7	28	28.2
Provident Financial	39.92	42.63	44.44	45.77	47.15	63.5	63.5	63.5	63.5
PZ Cussons	2.9	3.2	3.53	3.88	4.27	4.7	5.27	5.9	6.61
Reckitt Benckiser Group	25.5	28	34	39	45.5	55	80	100	115
Rentokil Initial	5.53	6.1	6.71	7.38	7.38	7.38	0.65	0	0
Stagecoach Group	2.69	3	3.39	3.8	4.1	5.4	6	6.5	7.1
Standard Chartered	24.62	24.57	25.83	30.06	30.63	33.5	40.88	41.23	43.97
Synergy Health	2.76	3.62	6	7	8.4	10.1	11	13.2	15.84
Taylor Wimpey	6.32	7.6	9.48	11.45	12.6	13.45	0	0	0
Tesco	6.2	6.84	7.56	8.63	9.64	10.9	11.96	13.05	14.46
Tullett Prebon	3.53	4.07	4.51	7.43	7.81	12	12.75	15	15.75
Unilever	35.64	40.18	42.56	45.13	47.66	51.11	60.74	41.26	71.24
Vodafone Group	1.69	2.03	4.07	6.06	6.76	7.51	7.77	8.31	8.9
Whitbread	19.98	22.42	25.39	28.06	30.25	36	36.55	38	44.5

We can see that, on the whole, most of the companies featured have managed to increase their dividend every year. Examples of the smooth upward movement we hope to see are Aggreko, Associated British Foods and Stagecoach. This is what dividend investors are looking for.

Sometimes dividends have lurched upwards sharply in a particularly good year. For instance, Centrica, although it increased the dividend every year, did particularly well by its shareholders six years ago, five years ago and three years ago. Vodafone shot ahead six and five years ago.

As long as these lurches are part of an overall upward trend we should welcome then as extra icing on the cake.

However, we do need to be alert to the possibility that a rising dividend can hit the buffers. Provident Financial was doing well until the financial crisis but the dividend has stuck for the past two years. This is not too bad. The dividend was raised sharply before the rises ceased and we are still getting a good payout. In these circumstances investors should monitor the company carefully to reassure themselves that the dividend can be maintained.

Rather more serious is the situation at house-builder Taylor Woodrow, where a steadily rising dividend came to an abrupt halt. As is so often the case, shareholders had adequate warning and had adequate opportunity to get out before the payouts dried up. The whole housing market was grinding to a halt in the light of the banking crisis and the mortgage famine.

Although dividend investing generally involves taking a long-term view, that is not an excuse to bury your head in the sand when things start to go wrong.

Occasionally, although this is unusual, we see dividends bouncing up and down year by year. Mining group Anglo American has a particularly erratic record. Such shares are unsuitable for an investor seeking solid dividend income.

Case study: Greggs

One of the best investments of the new millennium has been bakery chain Greggs, a prime example of how to run a successful retail group in what have been difficult times for the High Street generally.

For several years, revenue, profits, earnings per share and dividends maintained a steady although undramatic climb that is joy to the heart of the dividend investor. Companies with this kind of record are usually worthy but boring, yet there was nothing staid about Greggs.

Table 8.2 – Four-year financial history for Greggs

Calendar year	2008	2009	2010	2011[1]
Revenue (£m)	628	658	662	706
Pre-tax profits (£m)	49.5	48.8	52.5	55.4
Earnings per share (p)	30.7	34.1	37.8	39.6
Dividend (p)	14.9	16.6	18.2	19.2

Source: London Stock Exchange, Morngingstar Premium

It was a dynamic company with a clear strategy, expanding at a manageable rate. Greggs had a happy knack of creating new products without neglecting its best-selling lines. Opening new stores and expanding the wares on offer is a recipe for success.

Greggs cleverly positioned itself away from the trendy and expensive coffee shop sector where Starbucks, Costa Coffee and Caffe Nero were in direct competition. For every customer seeking a sophisticated strawberry skinny latte there are half a dozen craving a humble bacon roll.

The outlets gained a reputation for providing value for money, a policy that proved more sound than ever when the credit crunch started to bite and living standards fell as the new coalition government tackled the budget deficit.

---

[1]Forecast at time of 2010 results.

Greggs aimed originally at the lunch market with a range of sandwiches and cakes. Then chief executive Ken McMeikan saw an opportunity in the breakfast market selling bacon rolls plus tea or coffee. Catch the customers going into work as well as in their breaks and you have the potential to double your sales.

Bacon rolls soon led to porridge and McMeikan was not averse to eating into the more upmarket lines such as croissants, pains au chocolat and fruit smoothies.

You got the impression that Greggs knew what it was doing and it backed its own judgement with substantial capital expenditure: £30.3 million in 2009, £45.6 million in 2010 and £60 million in 2011.

This cash expanded the chain to nearly 1,600 outlets. Apart from snapping up vacant units cheaply in the High Street as other retailers failed, it moved into markets with a captive audience such as industrial estates, transport hubs and even football grounds.

It was by no means easy going. Greggs was affected as every other business was by rising costs of electricity, rents, council taxes and, particularly in 2010, by soaring prices for raw materials.

Producing much of what it sold did enable Greggs to maintain margins without raising prices to customers. One initiative was to reduce the amount of fresh food that had to be thrown away.

One further attraction of Greggs was that, despite 26 consecutive years of dividend increases, the share price frequently offered buying opportunities. During 2010 alone, the shares dipped to 450p in March and May, 420p in August, 430p in November and 435p in December compared with 500p in April.

Chart 8.1 – Share price of Greggs (GRG) (2009–11)

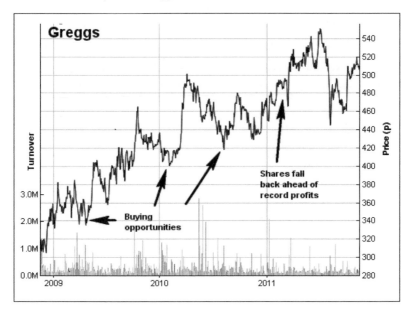

Between August 2009, when the stock market started to pick up after the credit crunch, and the publication of 2010 results in March 2011, Greggs shares had risen only 17% compared with a 20% gain in the FTSE 100 Index over the same period. That was scant reward for such a solid performance.

The shares had fallen back 25p to 466.25p in the run-up to those record profit figures yet they failed to respond on the day the results were released. At that point the forecast yield was an attractive 4% and the 2011 projections were dependent on nothing more than marginally positive growth in like-for-like sales, which were currently running 0.4% higher than a year earlier.

Those who stepped in while the going was good were soon rewarded as the shares belatedly responded with a gain to 514p a week later.

Key points

- The best investments are the ones where the company increases its dividend year by year.

- The past is not necessarily repeated but it is your best guide to how well the company is run.

- A progressive dividend policy is usually reflected in the share price but there will still be buying opportunities.

Chapter 9
Dividend Yield

A problem of comparing dividends

Let us take two very different companies, one making chemicals and the other food, and consider the total dividend that each paid per share in 2010-11:

- Johnson Matthey paid 46p

- Dairy Crest paid 19.7p

Which company would you prefer to buy?

The answer is that you cannot say. You would need to see a lot more information on the two companies, but we do have a starting point, and that is to find their respective yields, which will give us a direct comparison.

We start by finding the share prices of the two companies, taking 28 October 2011 as the date we were thinking of buying the shares:

Johnson Matthey's share price was £19.27, which looks quite a high price to pay for a 46p dividend.

Dairy Crest's share price was 350p, so although its dividend was less than half that of Johnson Matthey the company suddenly looks somewhat more attractive.

Calculating the dividend yield

The dividend yield is the most important calculation for dividend seekers, as it allows us to compare the dividends paid by different companies.

It is calculated by dividing the dividend per share by the share price, then multiplying by 100 to turn the answer into a percentage. The formula is:

$$\text{dividend yield} = \frac{\text{dividend}}{\text{share price}} \times 100$$

In the two examples above on the date in question:

- Johnson Matthey with a share price of £19.27p and a dividend of 46p has a yield of 2.4% (46/1927 x 100).

- Dairy Crest with a share price of 350p and a dividend of 19.7p has a yield of 5.6% (19.7/350 x 100).

So, we can now see that although Johnson Matthey has the higher dividend of 46p, the return is actually less. An investment in Dairy Crest would offer the better return based on dividends paid in the previous financial year.

What we have seen is that we cannot directly compare the dividends of companies. But we can compare the investment return on those dividends. These investment returns are usually called the 'dividend yield' (or simply 'the yield').

The yield tells you what annual return you can expect from your investment. It is the equivalent of the interest you receive on your savings account; so for a start you can immediately tell whether you are doing better than trusting your cash to the bank.

Units

When calculating dividend yield (and any ratio) it's important to make sure the units are consistent. In the example of Johnson Matthey, the share price was quoted in pounds (£19.27) while the dividend was quoted in pence (46p). To calculate the dividend yield it was therefore necessary to convert the share price to pence (1927p). You will find that share prices below £10 are normally quoted in pence; above £10 it is common to see the share price in pounds.

It is vital to use the total dividend paid during the financial year to get an accurate calculation. That will normally mean adding the interim dividend to the final, although it could mean adding together four quarterly payments.

You cannot calculate the annual yield halfway through the year by doubling the interim dividend because you are likely to get a false figure. The final dividend is often twice as large as the interim. Rarely are the two the same.

Clearly, as a general principle, the higher the yield the better. However, we still need to do a bit of homework. The yield may be high because other investors have overlooked the company's potential; alternatively there may be serious doubts about whether the company can maintain its dividend and these doubts have been factored into a very low share price.

A sample of some FTSE 350 companies and their dividend yield is given in the following table.

Table 9.1 – Dividend yields for a selection of FTSE 350 companies (26 Aug 2011)

Company	EPIC	Close	Dividend (p)	Yield (%)
Thomas Cook	TCG	43.33p	10.75	24.8
Cable & Wireless Worldwide	CW.	34.35p	4.5	13.1
Aviva	AV.	311.6p	25.5	8.2
Drax	DRX	487.7p	32	6.6
Greene King	GNK	425.8p	23.1	5.4
Daily Mail and General Trust	DMGT	380.1p	16	4.2
Restaurant Group	RTN	270.3p	9	3.3
Chemring	CHG	518p	11.7621	2.3
Burberry	BRBY	£12.57	20	1.6
Lonmin	LMI	£11.75	9.41	0.8
ARM Holdings	ARM	533p	2.9	0.5
Shire Pharmaceuticals	SHP	£19.21	8.14	0.4

We note that the yields vary enormously. As a very rough guide, yields on shares quoted on the London Stock Exchange tend to average somewhere around 3.5%. The figure is likely to be higher in times of high inflation and lower when inflation is steady but 3.5% is a good basis to work on.

We can see that in the table ARM and Shire offer very poor returns. As dividend investors we would shun then unless we can find compelling reasons to believe that returns will improve dramatically in the not too distant future.

In contrast, travel group Thomas Cook looks a fantastic bargain! However, while we want high yields, we must be suspicious if the yield looks too good to be true. It is a sign that the market believes the dividend, and therefore the yield, will be reduced sharply, and therefore the shares have been sold (and as the share price has fallen the calculated yield has increased). In the event, Thomas Cook soon suspended its dividend.

There are other factors to consider and we will analyse then in the next two chapters.

The dividend yield is always changing

It's important to remember that because dividend yields are dependent on the share price, the yield changes every time the share price changes. Let's look again at the formula for dividend yield:

$$\text{dividend yield} = \frac{\text{dividend}}{\text{share price}} \times 100$$

We can see that the calculated dividend yield is a function of two numbers:

1. **dividend**: this number will only change once a year when a new final dividend is paid (if we are using the historic dividend to calculate the yield)

2. **share price**: this number changes every day (sometimes every minute). If the share price falls then the calculated yield increases, and vice versa.

For example, the following table shows how the dividend yields for the companies in the above table would have looked if we had calculated them using the share price from a month before.

Table 9.2 – Comparison of calculated dividend yields for two different dates

Company	Yield (26/7/2011)	Yield (26/8/2011)
Thomas Cook	15.4	24.8
Cable & Wireless Worldwide	10.8	13.1
Aviva	6.2	8.2
Drax	6.1	6.6
Greene King	4.8	5.4
Daily Mail and General Trust	3.8	4.2
Restaurant Group	3.0	3.3
Chemring	2.1	2.3
Burberry	1.3	1.6
Lonmin	0.7	0.8
ARM Holdings	0.5	0.5
Shire	0.4	0.4

As you can see in some cases (e.g. ARM) the dividend yield changed little whether calculated on 26/7/2011 or 26/2011; this is because the share price was pretty much the same on those two dates. However, for other companies, the dividend yield changed greatly because the share price had moved significantly in the month between the two dates.

Two types of dividend yield

As we noted in the case of Thomas Cook in the table showing a selection of yields for FTSE 350 stocks, we are concerned not only about what dividends were in the latest financial year but also what is likely to happen in the next one.

Thus, the dividend yield may be calculated as:

1. *historic* or

2. *prospective* (sometimes referred to as *future* or *projected*).

We will look at each of these two in turn.

1. Historic

The historic figure is based on what dividend the company actually paid in its last complete financial year divided by the current share price.

While this has the advantage of using a known figure for the dividend, the calculation has several unsatisfactory aspects, not least the fact that the current share price reflects expectations for future performance rather than what happened in the past.

The final dividend will be declared at least a month after the end of the financial year, when there has been time to draw up the full-year accounts, and possibly three months later.

Companies quoted on AIM are allowed up to six months to complete their accounts and sometimes cannot manage even that extended time scale.

So you could be using one figure (the dividend) that is months old and another (the share price) that is literally up to the minute.

2. Prospective

The prospective yield is based on what dividend the company is expected to pay in the current and subsequent years. Serious investors will concentrate on the prospective figures on the grounds that a company is worth only as much as its next set of figures.

So, what we need are prospective figures for the upcoming dividend – but where do such figures come from?

Prospective figures are the forecasts of analysts, who are often employed by stock brokers. They are, therefore, forecasts, and not recorded facts, as historic figures are.

Analysts don't always get it right, and occasionally one can be sceptical of their efforts, but generally investors follow their forecast because:

- They specialise in analysing companies in a particular sector or region.

- They attend meetings with chairpeople and top executives when results are announced.

- They usually have ready access to these executives at other times if they want to clarify any issues arising.

- They need to be reasonably accurate or the broker loses credibility with clients paying for advice.

It is strictly against London Stock Exchange rules for company directors to give to analysts 'material' information – that is facts that could influence the company's share price – without also releasing the same information to the general public. Nonetheless it is highly advantageous to be able to quiz those directors on specific points.

We can assume, therefore, that forecasts are likely to be reasonably accurate. What is more, there are likely to be several analysts covering larger companies so we can obtain a consensus of forecasts.

With smaller companies there are likely to be only one or two analysts reporting and with the smallest companies, including many on AIM, there may be no coverage at all.

This is a bit of a nuisance when we try to take a view on an investment but it can be turned to your advantage. The less attention a company receives, the greater the possibility that it is not fully valued and therefore there may be an opportunity for investors who do their homework to pick up a bargain.

Where to find prospective yields

One serious problem with using prospective yields is the difficulty of finding them. Because analysts are paid to produce research, you may have to pay to get the most up-to-date figures.

If your stock broker produces research you can pay a fee to have this output sent to you but:

- you will be receiving just one broker's view on each company rather than a range of forecasts.

- you receive information on only those companies covered by the broker.

- the broker may cover only certain sectors or specialise in companies of a particular size.

Some financial websites do cover a range of forecasts. One of the best is Morningstar Premium (**www.morningstar.co.uk**). Call up any company and click on 'Stock Report PDF' to find a list of forecasts, who made them and when. The table looks like this:

Detailed Broker Forecast								
			2012			2013		
	Date	Rec	Pre-Tax	EPS	DPS	Pre-Tax	EPS	DPS
Panmure Gordon	03/01/2012	BUY	279	40.80	23.60	266	41.10	25.30
Peel Hunt	23/12/2011	HOLD	277	40.61	23.61	264	38.32	25.27
Shore Capital	23/12/2011	HOLD	269	40.00	23.60	281	40.90	25.30
Investec Securities	07/12/2011	BUY	274	40.10	23.66	260	37.64	25.32
The Royal Bank of Scotland NV	28/11/2011	BUY	267	39.52	23.67	261	40.27	25.33
Charles Stanley	04/11/2011	HOLD	336	49.50	23.50	345	51.00	24.50
Charles Stanley Securities	09/02/2011	REDU	308	45.32	23.09	333	49.30	24.86
Arbuthnot Securities	05/11/2009		-	-	-	376	55.40	-
Consensus			**274**	**40.28**	**23.62**	**267**	**39.64**	**25.30**
1m Change			+0	0.00	0.00	0	+0.03	0.00
3m Change			+3	+0.26	0.00	-12	-1.95	0.00

You can choose if you wish to ignore the house broker or those forecasts that are wildly out from the average or you can concentrate on the most recent forecasts.

This is, however, a paid-for service.

You can find a consensus forecast free on Digital Look (**www.digitallook.com**) but this does not give you the range of forecasts. *The Daily Telegraph* website (**www.telegraph.co.uk**) gives the average forecast plus the highest and lowest forecast.

Making your own calculations

You can work out your own forecast of the yield for the current financial year with some degree of accuracy. First, you can see if the dividend has been unchanged for the past three to five years or whether it has risen by the same percentage each time. This gives you some idea of what the dividend will be in future, assuming nothing dramatic happens.

Check trading statements since the last dividend was declared. If nothing untoward has happened, and particularly if the company consistently says that trading is in line with analysts' or market expectations, then the prevailing dividend policy will almost certainly continue.

Beware, however, the phrase claiming that trading is "in line with the board's expectations". This can actually be a signal that trading has taken a turn for the worse and can be a preliminary softening up before a profit warning. Check whether the company has actually said quite recently what the board's expectations are.

If the interim dividend has already been declared, see what percentage change, up or down, was made. It is likely that a similar percentage change will be made to the final dividend unless there has been an indication to the contrary. An unchanged interim is almost always followed by an unchanged final.

The main exception is where the company has said that it is "rebalancing" its dividend. It is possible over time for the interim to become comparatively very small or quite large compared to the final dividend. Possibly trading has become skewed with one half of the financial year much better than the other.

The company may decide to reset the dividends to a proportion that the board is more comfortable with. This will have been announced with previous results and the interim and full-year results will contain a reminder until the re-balancing is complete.

Comparing historic and prospective yields

A sample of some FTSE 350 companies comparing their historic with prospective dividend yields is given in Table 9.3.

Table 9.3 – Historic v prospective dividend yields for a selection of FTSE 350 companies (26 Aug 2011)

Company	EPIC	Historic Yield	Prospective yield
Catlin Group	CGL	7.6	7.8
BAE Systems	BA.	6.7	7.3
Centrica	CNA	4.8	5.1
TalkTalk Telecom	TALK	4.5	6.0
Moneysupermarket.com	MONY	3.5	6.3
Smith (DS)	SMDS	3.5	4.1
BHP Billiton	BLT	3.2	3.1
Wetherspoon (J D)	JDW	3.0	3.0
Homeserve	HSV	2.3	2.6
Aquarius Platinum	AQP	2.1	1.8
Invensys	ISYS	1.6	2.1

We naturally prefer companies where the prospective yield is higher than the historic yield. This means that the company is expected to increase its dividend.

In Table 9.3, BAE Systems is forecast to increase its dividend, thus boosting its already substantial yield. We can see that Moneysupermarket.com with a yield around the stock market average last time, is expected to boost its dividend, and yield, dramatically.

J D Wetherspoon is forecast to maintain its dividend at last year's level. Thus the historic and prospective yields are identical.

On the basis of this table, we would be concerned about BHP Billiton and Aquarius Platinum, where the yield is forecast to come in lower than before.

Rising yields

You may see an analyst's forecast of a yield of x%, rising to y% next year and z% the year after. This assumes that the dividend will increase year by year, which is the sort of company we are looking to invest in. Remember, however, that like the weather forecast, the further ahead that dividend forecasts go the less reliable they are. A lot can happen over two years.

That said, dividend forecasts are more accurate than most financial figures. While sales and profits can jump around, directors will try to keep the dividend steady or, preferably, rising gradually, so the better years provide reserves to cover the less fruitful ones.

Key points

- Dividend yield is the first, but by no means the only, calculation that dividend investors should make.

- Historic yields tell us what return we got last year; prospective returns are what we can hope to receive in future years.

- We are looking for companies with rising yields.

- As a general principle, we prefer to invest in companies with higher yields but we should be suspicious of shares that seem to offer very high yields.

Chapter 10
Other Key Ratios

Having looked at the most important ratio for dividend investors – the dividend yield – in the previous chapter, in this chapter we'll look at some other ratios that can be useful.

You will from time to time come across various ratios mentioned in the financial press, but it is not necessary to understand them all, just the ones that are particularly relevant to the payment of dividends.

Nor is it necessary to have an A level in maths. A simple grasp of basic sums will do. Ratios are simply one number divided by another.

Ratios are vital tools for investors. They help you to compare the performance of different companies. They can show whether a company is improving its performance, going backwards or standing still.

If you feel that you are an incomplete investor, without full knowledge of the range of ratios, then you should read *Ratios Made Simple*.[2] It contains all the main ratios and a few more besides, with an explanation of how to make the calculations and what use they are.

In this chapter we will look at the following ratios:

1. Earnings per share
2. Price/earnings ratio
3. Dividend cover
4. Gearing
5. Interest cover
6. Cash flow
7. Total return

---

[2] *Ratios Made Simple* by Robert Leach (Harriman House).

> ### Consolidated accounts
>
> One important point: Always use the Group/consolidated accounts if the Group has several subsidiaries. Group accounts contain all the figures pertaining to all the operations. These accounts are often called 'consolidated accounts' because all the figures for the separate subsidiaries are consolidated into one set of figures.
>
> You want the full picture provided by the Group/consolidated accounts.

1. Earnings per share

One of the most important figures we look at for any company is its profits (also referred to as earnings). However, accounting ratios are usually calculated on a per share basis, so we need to adjust the profit figure for this. To do this we divide the profit by the number of shares in issue – the resulting figure is called the earnings per share (EPS). The formula is:

$$\text{earnings per share} = \frac{\text{net profit}}{\text{number of shares in issue}}$$

Net profit is profit after interest, tax and minority interests but before the payment of dividends to ordinary shareholders. Everything has been paid for except your dividends. We shall see further on in this chapter that not all the earnings are paid out in dividends. Some, possibly all, cash will be retained for use in the business.

The EPS figure is used in a number of different ratios, which is why it is important, but do not be daunted by it. The figure *must* be included in company results so you do not have to calculate it for yourself.

A sample of some FTSE 350 with their FY2010 earnings per share is given in Table 10.1.

Table 10.1 – Earnings per share for a selection of FTSE 350 companies (FY2010)

Company	EPIC	EPS
Admiral	ADM	72.20p
Dignity	DTY	46.74p
Hiscox	HSX	45.05p
Invensys	ISYS	25.14p
Keller	KLR	42.42p
National Express	NEX	19.50p
Stagecoach	SGC	22.83p
Travis Perkins	TPK	70.05p
Witan Investment Trust	WTAN	9.45p

For example, in FY2010 we can see that Dignity had earnings per share of 46.74p.

There is not much that we can do with the EPS figure on its own (beyond compare it with those for previous years or forecasts). So, for example, referring to Table 10.1 we can't draw any particular conclusions by comparing the EPS figures of those different companies. But when we need to use a company's profit figure in a calculation, it is the EPS figure that we will use.

Complications with the EPS

So, the EPS looks a fairly simple calculation: just take the profit and divide that figure by the number of shares in issue. Unfortunately, there are complications.

Complication no. 1: profits

There can be problems over how we calculate profits. You may think that a profit is a profit is a profit, but attempts over the years to make the calculation of profits more meaningful have actually made them arguably more opaque.

The Accounting Standards Authority (ASA) has quite rightly clamped down on various schemes that inflated profits in the short term but were prone to produce nasty surprises in future years. Even now we get the occasional blip, usually in a badly controlled subsidiary, where revenue has been included in accounts before it has been received.

However, on the whole you can believe the profit figure you see in the Group accounts. If anything it is rigged towards understating profits because debts must be included as they are incurred, irrespective of when they are paid, while revenue does not count until the cash is in the finance director's mitt.

One important aspect of accounting regulations has been to insist that unusual large items are included in the profits calculation rather than classified separately as exceptional or extraordinary profits or losses.

So if a company decides to write off the value of assets, the hit will be taken in one year rather than spread over several periods. Similarly if the Group sells a subsidiary at a higher figure than it is valued at in the books, that profit goes into one year's accounts although the increase in value occurred over several years.

In most companies for most years this has little impact, but it can have spectacular consequences. Telecoms group Vodafone produced the biggest loss in UK corporate history when it wrote off the goodwill on its acquisition of German rival Mannesmann.

Banks such as Lloyds also produced multi-billion losses by writing off sub-prime mortgages and other bad debts.

It is also worth noting that where a company is going to incur a pre-tax loss by including exceptional items the directors are inclined to throw in every possible bad debt or writedown to get it all over in one go. This is known as 'kitchen sink accounting' and often happens when new management takes control.

The corollary is that some writeoffs prove unnecessary and the assets are written back into the accounts later, thus inflating the size of profits in future years.

Companies may therefore produce 'normalised profits' that strip out exceptional items in an attempt to provide meaningful comparisons year by year. This alternative calculation is sometimes given alongside the statutory EPS.

So which figure should we follow? As always, use your commonsense and look at figures over the past three to five years. Normalised EPS should give us a clearer picture of the trend and this is the figure we would usually prefer.

Complication no. 2: number of shares

Weighted number of shares

Companies may issue some shares during the course of the financial year, as incentives for executives, in rights issues, in share placings or to take over another company. Usually this will not make much difference to the earnings per share calculation but it can have a considerable effect if a large number of shares are issued.

Alternatively, the company may buy back shares, reducing the total number of shares in issue. This is a subject we shall deal with in a later chapter.

So should you divide earnings by the number of shares at the start of the year or at the end of the year? We can use a weighted figure, with shares already issued before the start of the year counting in full, those issued halfway through counting as only half a share, those issued a quarter of the way through the year as three-quarters of a share and so on.

Did your eyes glaze over there?

"Is it worth the effort?" did you ask? No, it isn't. Life is too short. If the company uses a weighted calculation, so be it. If you do the calculation yourself use the number of shares in issue at the *end* of the financial year.

Any dividends will probably be distributed among all the shares owned at year end and all future dividends certainly will be.

Diluted and undiluted

Apart from the shares actually issued, the company may have definite intentions to issue more shares. Perhaps directors have earned the right to subscribe for new shares at an advantageous price but have not yet done so. Or a company may have been acquired on the understanding that the previous owners will be issued shares if profits reach a certain level in future years.

The *undiluted* number of shares is the number actually issued. Quite rightly, this is the figure usually used in calculating EPS. It is, after all, the true number.

The *diluted* number of shares is the number that would have existed if all options had already been exercised or convertible shares had been converted. This figure may be relevant in future years but it is not a reality yet.

The diluted and undiluted figures are normally not much different anyway. There are far more important matters to concern yourself with so stick to the undiluted figure.

2. Price/earnings ratio

The price/earnings (P/E) ratio is one of the most popular and oft-touted ratios in the whole scheme of things. It is more important for those seeking to turn a quick profit by buying and selling shares rather than for long-term investors requiring income, but it is a useful guide to whether a company's shares are cheap and can help any investor to make a sensible decision before splashing out hard-earned cash.

The P/E is calculated by dividing the share price by earnings per share, so:

$$\text{earnings per ratio} = \frac{\text{share price}}{\text{earnings per share}}$$

The P/E is the most common way of valuing shares and is, on the whole, the best way of seeing how the market thinks a company will perform. Companies making a loss do not have a P/E.

Unlike yield, where we look for a higher figure, we would prefer a lower P/E, which suggests that the shares are cheap. As with yield, the P/E allows us to compare companies of different sizes in different lines of business, or to compare a company with its peers in the same sector, or to see how a company is rated against the stock market as a whole.

The average P/E for the UK market tends to settle around 13-14 but it depends on the outlook for the economy. Many companies, including sound ones, were down to single figures in the recession.

Below 10 does indicate that investors feel some concern about the company. There is an implication that profits may fall short of expectations or that analysts may reduce their forecasts, which would push the P/E higher.

P/Es above 20 emerge if the economy is growing quickly. There are clearly high expectations for any company with a P/E above 18, expectations that may be difficult to fulfil.

Above 30 you should be very cautious. The bubble may burst. In particular beware of new companies coming to market with high prospective P/Es.

A sample of some FTSE 100 companies and their price/earnings ratios is given in Table 10.2.

Table 10.2 – P/Es for a selection of FTSE 100 companies (24 Aug 2011)

Company	EPIC	Price (p)	EPS (p)	P/E
ARM Holdings	ARM	530	6.4	82.3
Hargreaves Lansdown	HL.	425.4	13.9	30.7
SABMiller	SAB	2124	104.7	20.3
Unilever	ULVR	2043	133.4	15.3
Standard Chartered	STAN	1335	121.3	11.0
Vodafone Group	VOD	168	21.2	7.9
AstraZeneca	AZN	2873.5	418.1	6.9
Scottish & Southern Energy	SSE	1265	226.9	5.6
Aviva	AV.	327.4	67.1	4.9

We can see in this table that Unilever and Standard Chartered are roughly in line with the norm, with the latter looking the slightly more attractive proposition on this basis.

Four companies are in single figures, implying that they are either undervalued or there are concerns about future earnings. Aviva is on such a low P/E that we would want to make further investigations into why it has such an undemanding rating. There must be factors that are scaring off investors. The implication is that the market is doubtful of its ability to meet earnings forecasts.

In contrast, ARM Holdings is on such a massive rating that we wonder why it is so highly thought of. The implication is that investors believe that earnings will outpace expectations and really take off in the longer term. The possibility that ARM will fall short of such high hopes is considerable.

Hargreaves Lansdown is at the point where we should be very cautious and, to a lesser extent, we should be wary of SAB Miller unless we find particularly good grounds for investing.

Changes to P/E

As with yield, the P/E changes every time the share price moves, although you would not expect a significant change within a trading day unless something dramatic has happened, such as the issuing of a profit warning or the declaration of a takeover offer.

The calculation appears in those morning newspapers that carry stock market tables, with the *Financial Times* having the most extensive list of companies. These are based on the mid-market share price at the close of the previous trading day and it is easiest to work on the same basis if you want to make your own calculation. If you are a stickler for exactitude then by all means do a quick calculation based on the price you will actually pay for a holding.

Do remember that P/E is not such a big deal for dividend investors. You are concerned about how high the dividend will be rather than whether the share price will leap or collapse. However, a particularly low P/E should alert you to the possibility that all is not as it seems at the company and you should dig deeper to see whether the concerns are justified.

3. Dividend cover

This ratio tells you how safe the dividend is. It is used to establish if the dividend is under threat or whether there is scope for a dividend increase next year.

Dividend cover means how well each year's dividend is covered by that year's profits. You calculate it by dividing earnings per share by the dividend per share. The formula can be expressed thus:

$$\text{dividend cover} = \frac{\text{earnings per share}}{\text{dividend}}$$

For example, at the time of writing, Tesco in its latest full year had an EPS of 27.85p and had paid a total dividend of 14.46p, its dividend cover was therefore

$$\text{dividend cover} = \frac{27.85}{14.46} = 1.9$$

The higher the figure, the safer the dividend. There is more leeway to maintain the dividend if profits fall next year.

Dividend cover of 2 is regarded as the norm, which means that half the profits are paid in dividends and half are reinvested, although this is a rule of thumb rather than a hard and fast requirement.

Any figure over 2 suggests that there is scope for a 'progressive' dividend policy, that is one where the dividend is increased each year.

It is possible for the dividend cover to drop below 2 for one or two years without damaging the prospects of a progressive dividend. This is particularly true if profits are reduced, or even wiped out, by extraordinary losses such as an asset writedown, provided we are satisfied that this is a one-off setback.

Any figure that is less than 1 means that at least part of the dividend is being paid out of reserves. If the company makes a loss there is no dividend cover and any dividend will have to be paid totally out of reserves. Once the reserves, which are past profits that have been saved, are exhausted, then no further dividends can be paid until the company returns to profit and any accumulated loses have been wiped out.

A sample of some FTSE 100 companies and their dividend cover is given in Table 10.3.

Table 10.3 – Dividend cover for a selection of FTSE 100 companies (24 Aug 2011)

Company	EPIC	EPS	Dividend	Cover
GKN	GKN	17.9	5.0	3.6
Aviva	AV.	67.1	25.5	2.6
Marks & Spencer	MKS	39.7	17.0	2.3
International Power	IPR	21.9	10.9	2.0
Diageo	DGE	69.6	38.1	1.8
Reed Elsevier	REL	32.4	20.4	1.6
United Utilities	UU.	40.7	30.0	1.4
GlaxoSmithKline	GSK	59.8	65.0	0.9

With a dividend cover of 3.6, GKN seems to be erring on the side of caution. That is no bad thing and it does mean that there is a strong possibility of increases in the dividend in future years. Aviva's dividend is also well covered, which makes the lowly P/E rating that we noted earlier in this chapter all the more surprising.

Marks & Spencer and International Power are around the norm, so there is no cause for concern. However, Diageo and Reed Elsevier have slipped below what is normally regarded as safe and we would want to look closely at whether the dividend is in any danger or whether this is a short-term blip.

United Utilities has slipped even further but the biggest worry is at Glaxo, where earnings failed to cover the dividend fully and the pharmaceuticals group is dipping into reserves to maintain the payment.

If the dividend cover is declining each year, then the company is struggling to maintain the dividend at its present level. Directors are very reluctant to suffer the ignominy of recommending a reduced dividend so this situation may continue for two or three years before reality prevails.

If we are unlucky, the dividend will be scrapped. If we are lucky, the dividend will be 're-based', which is a euphemism for slashing it in the hope that it can be slowly increased from a lower level.

Where a dividend is re-based, check what the cover is for the new dividend. It should be comfortably over 2 to allow for further mishaps. The board will not want to cut the payout again so it is likely that the re-based dividend is sustainable.

Dividend payout ratio

This is the flip side of dividend cover. If you understand this more easily than dividend cover, fine. Otherwise dividend cover is the better tool to use.

The payout ratio is calculated by dividing the dividend per share by earnings per share. This tells you how much of available profit is passed to shareholders rather than retained in the company for investment. The formula for the payout ratio is:

$$\text{dividend cover} = \frac{\text{dividend}}{\text{earnings per share}}$$

Taking the same example of Tesco as before, its payout ratio would be:

$$\text{payout ratio} = \frac{14.46}{27.85} = 0.52$$

If you recall, we calculated the dividend cover for Tesco as 1.9, which is the reciprocal of 0.52:

$$1.9 = \frac{1}{0.52}$$

Just as the norm for dividend cover is 2, so turning the equation upside down gives us a norm of 0.5. The higher the figure, the greater the proportion of earnings that are being paid out in dividends. A lower figure indicates that the dividend is more secure and there will also be scope for capital growth.

A ratio of more than 1 means that at least part of the dividend has been paid out of reserves.

As a dividend investor you may prefer a company with a ratio above rather than below 0.5 as you would prefer a company with a policy of rewarding shareholders as far as possible. However, do not be dogmatic.

A consistently high payout ratio could indicate an unsustainable dividend. Keeping cash to invest in the business could enable a company to increase dividends more rapidly in future.

4. Gearing (also referred to as leverage)

A cause for concern is high gearing, where there is a danger that the company has borrowed so heavily that cash will be channelled into interest payments to the bank rather than into dividends for investors.

Gearing is calculated by dividing total borrowings minus cash by shareholders' funds. The answer is multiplied by 100 to turn it into a percentage.

The higher the figure, then potentially the company is overstretched. The lower the figure the less the interest burden will be.

Shareholders' funds comprises the money that shareholders paid into the company when the shares were originally issued plus retained profits, that is profits that have been kept in the company rather than paid out in dividends. The figure will be reduced by any losses the company makes.

Debts include not only bank borrowings but also company bonds and preference shares. Bonds are simply money borrowed from the public rather than the banks and the rate of interest is set when they are issued rather than subject to the vagaries of the company's banker but they are clearly debt nonetheless.

Preference shares also have a set rate of interest that has to be paid each year before any money can be distributed as dividends on ordinary shares.

From these debts we can deduct any cash kept in a bank account or held on the premises.

There is no set level for gearing nor even a guide level at which alarm bells should start ringing. You would normally expect gearing to be less than 100%, but companies with particularly high capital costs, such as plant hire or construction groups, always have high gearing, usually above 100%.

The effect of gearing

Increasing and decreasing gearing comes in and out of fashion. High gearing means that the company's performance is magnified for better or worse so it comes into fashion when interest rates are low and economic prospects are improving.

When interest rates rise, making debt more expensive, and profits slip, making it harder to pay the interest, gearing loses its appeal. However, in these circumstances it becomes correspondingly difficult to generate enough cash to reduce gearing, which hangs like a millstone.

Interest on debt has to be paid whether the company is profitable or not and it is paid ahead of dividends. What is more, the debt itself has to be repaid some day. It has a finite life. If a debt has to be rolled over there may be tougher terms and bank fees.

The message is that, on the whole, highly geared companies are too high risk for income investors. It is true that, because they are seen as higher risk, the shares may be undervalued but this is not the sort of risk you want to be taking.

Dividends of highly geared companies may well be suspended in any economic downturn.

To say, as many companies do, that increased gearing makes the balance sheet more efficient is rubbish. As a dividend investor you should be particularly sceptical of any board of directors perpetrating this nonsense. They may actually believe it is true.

5. Interest cover

A company's borrowings naturally incur interest payments, which may be more or less onerous according to a variety of factors:

- how free or tight credit was when the loan was taken out

- how sound the company looked to its lenders

- how desperate the company was for cash when it took out the loan

- whether the company has a good record of repaying debt

- whether the company has previously broken its banking covenants (the terms on which the loans are granted).

Since interest on loans is paid before dividends, we want to know whether there is enough cash left over for us. Thus we need to calculate the level of interest cover, that is how well profits cover interest payments.

Interest cover is calculated by dividing earnings before interest and tax (referred to as EBIT) by the amount of interest paid. So, the formula is:

$$\text{interest cover} = \frac{\text{earnings before interest and tax}}{\text{interest paid}}$$

The higher the interest cover, the less troubled a company is by its debt burden. If a company has no debt then this calculation is impossible and irrelevant.

As a general principle, from 2 to 3 is seen as the norm while 1.5 is generally considered the bare minimum level of comfort for any company in any industry.

Less than 1 is bad news as profits are not covering the interest payments. Anyone who has ever borrowed from a bank knows that they don't like it if you can't pay the interest on loans. Neither do bond holders.

For companies with consistent revenues and profits, such as a utility company, an interest cover of 2 is an acceptable standard. This is particularly true where there is good visibility of earnings such as where a company's revenue comes from long-term contracts, especially if these are with the Government.

For more volatile industries, such as vehicle manufacturing or steel production, an acceptable minimum for interest coverage is 3. A greater margin of safety is required to ensure the company can cover interest charges during periods when earnings are down.

If you are super-cautious – which is no bad thing – you will prefer interest to be covered four times or more so that you can be confident that there is cash left to pay dividends and to invest in the business.

A sample of some FTSE 350 companies and their interest cover is given in Table 10.4.

Table 10.4 – Interest cover for a selection of FTSE 350 companies (24 Aug 2011)

Company	EPIC	Interest cover
Inchcape	INCH	12.20
Marks & Spencer	MKS	6.72
TUI Travel	TT.	4.03
Dignity	DTY	3.00
International Power	IPR	2.03
Segro	SGRO	2.00
Taylor Wimpey	TW.	1.44
Premier Foods	PFD	1.34
Enterprise Inns	ETI	1.10
Redrow	RDW	1.06
Capital Shopping Centres	CSCG	0.96
Grainger	GRI	0.70
Kenmare Resources	KMR	0.61
Mitchells & Butlers	MAB	0.43

There are clearly no worries about Inchcape paying its debts and Marks & Spencer has the debt imposition covered very comfortably. There are no obvious worries at TUI Travel and Dignity.

We would want to keep an eye on the situation at International Power and Segro, although there are no serious problems in paying interest at this stage.

Dividend cover has fallen too far for comfort at Taylor Wimpey and Premier Foods and there are serious concerns over whether Redrow will be able to keep paying the interest on its debts.

The bottom four companies in our table are not earning enough in profits to cover the interest on debt, a situation that cannot be allowed to persist. It means that they are drawing on reserves to cover interest and that dividends will not be possible unless the deficit is rectified.

6. Cash flow

Your dividend is paid out of the cash that the company earns or has squirreled away so you are naturally interested in whether cash is flowing in or out of the company.

There is no need to calculate cash flow. This figure is given in the results. As you would expect, a positive figure is simply net cash coming into the business while a negative figure means an outward cash flow.

Cash is king. Unless cash starts flowing in, a company can stay in business for only so long, let alone meet interest on loans or pay a dividend. So the higher the positive figure, or at least the lower the negative figure, the better.

Factors affecting cash flow include:

- cash flow from operating activities
- returns on investments
- taxation
- capital expenditure.

If there is an outflow, you should consider whether this is a one-off deficit or a long-term malaise.

The problem with cash flow is that heavy spending on plant or equipment can distort one year's figures. This is less of an issue with large companies, where heavy capital spending goes on all the time and figures tend to roughly balance out from year to year. With smaller companies capital spending tends to be more lumpy, so it is no surprise if heavy investment one year knocks cash flow for six.

Yet, on the whole, we want companies to invest, since future profits and cash flow depend on up-to-date computer systems or manufacturing processes.

It is sensible to check cash flow over the past three to five years to get a clear picture. A sample of some FTSE 100 companies and their cash flows for the past five years in given in Table 10.5.

Table 10.5 – Historic cash flow for a selection of FTSE 100 companies (2011)

Company	EPIC	Cash flow – most recent (£m)	Cash flow – 1 year ago (£m)	Cash flow – 2 years ago (£m)	Cash flow – 3 years ago (£m)	Cash flow – 4 years ago (£m)
BT	BT.A	3,630	3,880	3,830	4,780	4,530
Capital Shopping Centres	CSCG	-287	80	86	42	115
GKN	GKN	40	218	301	249	53
Kingfisher	KGF	617	1,070	1,250	384	506
Marks & Spencer	MKS	1,060	1,070	1,110	986	1,160
Next	NXT	431	540	400	482	472
Reed Elsevier	REL	585	-6	489	829	585
Smith & Nephew	SN.	549	445	388	218	189
Smiths Group	SMIN	410	332	192	2,740	556
Vodafone	VOD	13,600	13,200	11,800	10,300	7,360

There are certainly no worries at Vodafone and at Smith & Nephew, where cash flow has risen year by year. Such a steady rise is, however, unusual and we would not be at all concerned about the situation at Next or Marks & Spencer, where cash flow has remained positive and fairly steady.

Reed Elsevier dipped into negative cash flow in the 1 year ago column but this looks to be a temporary blip with the latest figure back in positive territory. The Group can easily stand such a tiny outflow in one year out of five.

Capital Shopping Centres needs closer inspection as a strong cash outflow in the latest year has virtually wiped out the inflows of the previous four years. We must, however, make allowances for the different types of business in our table. Companies that may incur heavy capital spending will inevitably have more lumpy cash flows.

Two alternative methods of calculating cash flow have been invented in an attempt to produce a more accurate picture. Unfortunately these are complicated and are not normally calculated for you by the company, although 'free cash flow' is sometimes included in results statements.

When this happens, just check that the company is not trying to distract you from a serious negative cash flow by drawing your attention to a more favourable calculation.

Free cash flow

This concept is an attempt to smooth out the vagaries of capital expenditure. So you include depreciation in the calculation but exclude capital spending.

Free cash flow is the amount that could be paid in dividends if the company paid out as much as possible without running down the operations or increasing debt.

Some investors think that free cash flow is a vital investment tool; others fear that life is too short for such obsessions that take all the fun out of investing.

Do not worry too much about minute detail. The important question is whether capital spending is being put to good use and whether, year on year, cash flow is positive or is heading that way.

Discounted cash flow

This is cash flow over several years adjusted for inflation. You may ask yourself what is the point of this dubious exercise.

Cash gone is cash gone, irrespective of inflation. If you are trying to calculate prospects for the future, how can you possibly know what inflation is going to be? It has become increasingly obvious that the Governor of the Bank of England does not know and he has more bean counters at his disposal than you have.

7. Total return

If you understand yield and dividend cover you have grasped the two ratios that are vital for dividend investors. However, it is recommended that you also comprehend the principle of *total return* on your investment.

Your total return is capital growth plus dividend. Let's take the example of calculating the total return for investing in Reckitt Benckiser shares in 2010.

In 2010 Reckitt Benckiser shares rose from £33.49 at the beginning of the year to £35.25 at the end. The capital growth was £1.76 (£35.25 - £33.49) and the return was:

$$\text{payout ratio} = \frac{(£35.25 - £33.49}{£33.49} = 5.3\%$$

However, an investor would also have received dividends from Reckitt Benckiser shares in 2010. In this year, the interim dividend was 50p and the final dividend was 65p, giving a total dividend of £1.15.

To calculate the total return, we need to add this dividend to the increased value of the shares, which gives £36.40 (£35.25 + £1.15). So, the investment per share has grown from £33.49 at the beginning of the year to £36.40 at the end of the year, which gives a total return of:

$$\text{total return} = \frac{(£36.40 - £33.49}{£33.49} = 8.7\%$$

The general formula for calculating total return is:

$$\text{total return} = \frac{(\text{share price at end of period + dividends} - \text{share price at start of period})}{\text{share price at start of period}}$$

Capital gains are not the *raison d'etre* of income investors. Nonetheless, it is always best to be realistic when investing in the stock market and total return gives you the most accurate picture of how well you have done.

Total return allows you to compare shares with other types of investment, such as gold that gives you a capital gain but no income, or a savings account that gives you income but no capital gain.

Key points

- Yield and dividend cover are the two most important calculations for dividend investors.

- Look for companies with at least two times dividend cover as they are more likely to be able to increase the dividend while still retaining enough cash to develop the business.

- You should also understand cash flow and interest cover.

- Prefer companies with earnings that cover interest payments at least three times, as debt will be less likely to be a problem.

- Dividends are paid out of a steady inward cash flow but do not be alarmed if the flow varies from year to year just as long as, overall, money is flowing in rather than out.

- It is not vital to understand all the other ratios but the more you grasp the better.

PART C

Investing Tactics

Chapter 11
Picking Sectors

So far we have looked at dividend investing mainly from the point of view of analysing companies to find the ones that look to be solid or promising investments.

Choosing companies, then seeing if there are any problems with the type of product they offer, or the sector they are in, or the markets they serve, is known as a bottom-up approach.

As a whole, this approach tends to suit private investors. The less sophisticated you are as an investor, the easier it is for you to grasp the merits or flaws of an individual company rather than an entire sector or market. It is fine if this is your approach – many highly experienced fund managers, possibly the majority, are bottom-up investors.

Some fund managers, however, prefer a top-down approach, looking at the most promising geographical areas first, then finding the best types of products and gradually narrowing the search down to the best company producing the best product in the best sector in the best market.

As always in investing, stick with what you feel most comfortable with.

The danger of bottom-up investing is that you may end up with several companies in the same sector and your income will suffer if that sector is hit by adverse economic conditions.

A top-down approach steers you away from this danger because, having picked the best company in one particular sector, you look at other sectors.

Whatever your approach, you should be aware that some sectors are more suitable than others for longer-term investing.

Cyclicals v Defensives

Cyclicals

These are the sectors whose fortunes ride up and down in line with the economy, increasing their profits and dividends in the good times but suffering in the downturns. They are called *cyclicals* because they follow the economic cycle.

Examples are manufacturing, leisure, most retailing especially furniture, and house building.

Cyclical sectors are for:

- shorter-term traders
- investors looking to spot opportunities for capital gains to augment dividends
- those who do not yet need a steady stream of income
- investors who are less averse to taking risks.

Defensives

These sectors sell pretty much the same amount of goods and services whatever the state of the economy. They do not enjoy the boom times as cyclical sectors do but neither are they set back so badly in tougher times. They are referred to as 'defensive stocks' because they are seen as a line of defence when your portfolio is under attack from falling share prices. Examples would include pharmaceuticals, tobacco, food, utilities and household goods.

Defensive sectors are for:

- less active investors
- those who need a steady stream of income
- investors who prefer to hold shares for the long term
- those who are averse to taking risks.

Dividend data by sector

Table 11.1 – Sector dividends (28 Aug 2011)

Sector	Historic Yield (avg)	Dividend cover (avg)	Projected yield (avg)
Aerospace & Defence	3.0	2.9	3.4
Automobiles & Parts	2.7	3.6	3.6
Banks	3.8	2.4	4.5
Beverages	3.4	2.2	3.6
Chemicals	2.1	3.6	2.8
Construction & Materials	5.7	2.0	5.8
Electricity	6.3	2.3	5.7
Electronic & Electrical Equipment	2.9	2.2	3.3
Financial Services	4.2	2.2	4.8
Fixed Line Telecommunications	8.2	1.7	8.1
Food & Drug Retailers	3.8	2.1	4.1
Food Producers	3.8	2.3	4.0
Forestry & Paper	3.5	2.3	4.3
Gas, Water & Multiutilities	4.4	1.9	4.7
General Industrials	3.3	3.1	4.2
General Retailers	4.4	2.9	4.5
Health Care Equipment & Services	1.7	3.7	1.9
Household Goods & Home Construction	2.0	3.6	2.0
Industrial Engineering	2.7	2.6	3.1
Industrial Metals & Mining	1.2	10.8	1.2
Industrial Transportation	4.9	1.7	5.0
Life Insurance	5.5	2.6	6.1
Media	3.5	1.9	3.9
Mining	1.9	5.2	1.6
Mobile Telecommunications	5.4	2.0	5.7
Nonlife Insurance	5.3	3.5	6.0
Oil & Gas Producers	2.2	2.1	2.9
Oil Equipment, Services & Distribution	2.3	2.5	2.5
Personal Goods	1.8	2.4	1.8
Pharmaceuticals & Biotechnology	2.8	4.0	2.9
Real Estate Investment Trusts	3.8	2.5	3.5
Software & Computer Services	2.8	3.3	3.1
Support Services	3.5	2.1	3.6
Technology Hardware & Equipment	1.5	7.5	1.7
Tobacco	4.2	1.7	4.7
Travel & Leisure	4.8	3.1	4.5

We can see that in the most recent financial year there were enormous variations in yields, ranging from a stingy 1.5% in Technology Hardware & Equipment to a juicy 8.2% in Fixed Line Telecommunications.

Dividend cover varied to an even greater extent, with five sectors averaging less than the two times what is normally regarded as comfortable. Industrial Metals & Mining looks safe but boring with cover way up in super-cautious double figures.

Most sectors are predicted to increase their dividends in the current financial year with the projected yield figures generally higher than those for historic yield. Electricity and Mining are two exceptions that should have us taking a cautious approach to companies in those sectors. Fixed Line Telecommunications is also projected to ease back but the yield will still be easily the best on offer.

We must bear in mind, however, that these are average figures. We need to look at individual companies to see whether they fit into the sector pattern.

Visibility of earnings

Some companies have what is referred to as 'good visibility of earnings'. That means you can see where the income is coming from for months or, preferably, years ahead.

A defensive company will tend to have good visibility of earnings. You know that contracts have been signed to provide work over a period of time so the income is guaranteed (provided the client does not go bust). Where those contracts are for government and local authority schemes you can be pretty sure that they will be honoured.

For instance, a contract to build a school will provide work for a building company for several months; a contract to maintain the school will provide work for several years.

Other companies live more hand-to-mouth. Generally speaking they sell to the general public whose spending patterns are more susceptible to economic change. In particular, items that we can manage without will be postponed indefinitely and possibly even be cancelled.

If we normally change our car every three or four years we can choose instead at the end of this period to have our car serviced and soldier on. If we delay long enough we can actually skip the new car purchase and buy after six or seven years, so the intervening purchase we would normally have made is lost forever.

Lumpy earnings

Sectors where earnings and expenses are lumpy should send a warning signal to dividend investors. This is especially so where costs and profits are largely outside the control of the companies operating in those sectors.

Two that spring immediately to mind are insurance and gambling.

Who knows when a natural disaster will break or when an outsider will win the Derby? Indeed, these sectors depend heavily on the elements of chance that bedevil or brighten up our daily lives.

Yet these operations need the occasional highly publicised heavy payout to tempt punters to hedge their bets or chance their arms.

Insurance

The 2010 calendar year proved to be a particularly tough one for insurers – with Lloyd's of London, the major reinsurance market, reckoning claims had topped £10 billion – and 2011 began with more of the same as an earthquake shattered the New Zealand city of Christchurch.

The Chilean earthquake that left 33 miners trapped underground for weeks may have been ultimately a stirring triumph of human endeavour over the forces of nature but it was still the costliest disaster of 2010 for insurers at the best part of £1 billion.

Elsewhere, in what was a disastrous year for many in the Southern Hemisphere, there were floods and fires in Australia. Then there were hurricanes in the Northern Hemisphere and the BP oil rig blow out in the Gulf of Mexico.

Events in New Zealand demonstrated how uncertain the insurance industry can be. A larger earthquake in September was deeper underground and caused no loss of life while a lesser aftershock five months later killed dozens of people because it was nearer the earth's surface and happened at midday when more people were out and about.

Consequently the second earthquake was likely to cost more than the first – and by that stage estimates of the cost of the September disaster had already risen to £3.5 billion.

And here is another point about insurance: initial estimates are always too low. Insurance companies seem to prefer to start with unrealistic optimism rather than assess a worst-case scenario that gives scope for scaling back estimates rather than ratcheting them up.

Then came the highly destructive tsunami in Japan, with whole towns washed away and a nuclear power station going into meltdown. It was obvious from the start that this would prove highly expensive, not just in human lives but also in financial costs. Initial estimates of the cost to Lloyd's of London again proved woefully inadequate and trebled within days to more than £20 billion.

The insurance industry was already facing a bleak year given that claims can roll in up to three years after the event and it was highly likely that the cost of the 2010 claims had been underestimated.

Case study: Amlin

Amlin was one of the Lloyd's insurers to suffer as the heavy claims rolled in. It saw pre-tax profits for 2010 fall 49% to £259.2 million as it incurred losses of £203.6 million from earthquakes in Chile and New Zealand.

The insurer did raise its final dividend by 15% to 23% on the basis that it had put in 'a highly creditable' performance at what it believed was the trough of the insurance trading cycle.

However, the results came out just before disaster struck Japan. By April Amlin was admitting that it faced catastrophe losses of up to £275 million for the first quarter of 2011 with the tsunami accounting for £150 million, New Zealand's earthquake £100 million and flooding in Australia £15 million.

One has to admit that Amlin had done reasonably well on the whole over several years, although profits bounced around, from £445 million in 2007 down to £122 million in 2008, then up to £509 million in 2009 before the sharp fall in 2010.

Despite these fluctuations, the dividend had been increased each year over that period and was forecast to rise to more than 24p for 2011.

Table 11.2 – Dividend history for Amlin

Calendar year	2006	2007	2008	2009	2010
Pre-tax profit	£342.7m	£445m	£121.6m	£509.1m	£259.2m
EPS	50.4p	68.8p	17.1p	94.1p	45.0p
Dividend	12.0p	15.0p	17.0p	20.0p	23.0p
Dividend cover	4.2	4.59	1.01	4.7	1.96

Source: London Stock Exchange

This was all very tempting and a sharp fall in the share price in March 2011 meant the shares were on a very attractive prospective yield of 6.3%, higher than the average of 6% for the sector and just under 4% for the London market as a whole.

The shares had been highly volatile, which provided ample opportunities for short- and medium-term traders to make profits. However, dividend investors had to weigh up whether they could stand the risks.

Chart 11.1 – Share price chart for Amlin

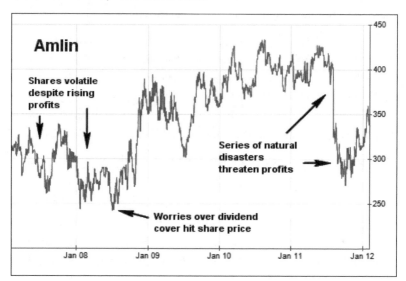

One key factor was dividend cover, which had been maintained at comparatively high levels in most years – well over four times in 2007 and 2009 – but had slumped in 2008 to the point where the dividend was barely covered.

Disaster insurance is admittedly the most lumpy of the insurance sectors because it involves fewer but larger claims. Household and motor insurance meets more frequent but smaller claims. Even so, premiums tend to go in cycles as new insurance companies are tempted in when premiums rise and are squeezed out as claims roll in.

Ambulance chasing and the rise of the litigious society have bumped up the cost of settling claims, particularly for motor insurance.

The most stable part of insurance is life insurance which tends to produce steady income and comparatively predictable costs.

Case study: Admiral

One should not lose sight of the possibility that, within a sector depending heavily on managing risk, there can be solid performers. Such companies can present a conundrum: even the best run companies are unable to avoid entirely the vagaries of the sector in which they operate so we need to be especially vigilant. It is important always to maintain common sense and flexibility.

Insurance group Admiral carved out a niche in the highly competitive UK car insurance market, managing to grow profits and dividends year by year. Indeed, the growth in dividends was quite spectacular.

Table 11.3 – Dividend history for Admiral

Calendar year	2008	2009	2010	2011 forecast
Revenue	£301m	£386m	£575m	£607m
Pre-tax profit	£203m	£216m	£266m	£306m
EPS	54.9p	59p	72.3p	83p
Dividend	24.7p	26.5p	50.6p	74.9p

Source: *Daily Telegraph*

The figures in the table were the culmination of seven years of record profits, a trend that looked set to continue. Admiral's revenue (the UK motor business accounting for 90% of it) outperformed established rivals such as Churchill and Direct Line, reaching the point where it insured one in ten British drivers.

Risk was alleviated through large reinsurers.

Admiral also operated the Confused.com price comparison website, where profits were falling, and had some loss-making overseas businesses. This exposure was reduced in 2010 by the sale of the German insurance arm.

Chart 11.2 – Share price chart for Admiral

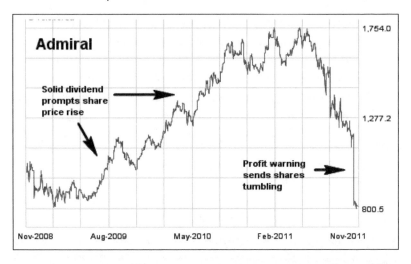

The great progress that Admiral made was reflected in the share price over the years. In particular, the shares soared from just over 1200p after the 2009 results to 1655p a year later.

Even so, the yield was just over 3% based on 2010 earnings, rising to 4.5% assuming that forecasts for 2011 were accurate.

Furthermore, a European Court ruling that motoring premiums could not be based on gender would boost earnings in 2012, since the unfortunate affect would be to prompt a rise in premiums for female drivers who had hitherto been rewarded for having fewer and less serious accidents.

In the event, life got tougher for Admiral in the later half of the year and although third quarter turnover jumped 30% in the third quarter Admiral's interim management statement issued on 9 November included a warning that record levels of personal injury claims meant that full-year profits were likely to be at the bottom end of the range of forecasts, although that would still leave them 10% higher than in the previous year.

Admiral shares fell 29% that day, from 1193p to 887.5p, presenting a buying opportunity for risk-takers hoping that the dividend would nonetheless be maintained. Two days later Chief Operating Officer David Stevens bought 225,000 shares at 826p each and although the share price continued to slide below 800p a week later it began a slow recovery to 840p by the end of the month.

Key points

- Some sectors are more likely to produce smoother, solid growth than others.

- Companies within the same sector may have completely different characteristics.

- If you buy cyclical shares on the upturn you should be prepared to bail out when the economic cycle turns down again.

- Defensive stocks are generally more suitable for dividend investors, especially those needing regular reliable income.

Chapter 12
Dividends by Index

It is not only sectors that we need to bear in mind when searching for the best investment opportunities; companies in the various indices have different dividend-paying profiles.

On the whole, larger companies are more likely to pay dividends than smaller ones and companies with a full listing on the London Stock Exchange are more likely to pay dividends than those on AIM.

Smaller companies on the whole take longer to pay up and they are also more likely to scrap their dividend, especially if their shares are quoted on AIM.

This is a general guide and there are perfectly sound, dividend-paying companies to be found in the FTSE Small Cap and FTSE Fledgling indices, often offering higher yields to reflect the great risk.

Table 12.1 – Dividend profiles for the various indices (28 Aug 2011)

	Dividend payers (%)	Average yield	Average dividend cover	Average payment date
FTSE 100	92	3.3	2.8	24/05/2011
FTSE 250	79	3.6	2.6	28/05/2011
FTSE 350	83	3.5	2.6	26/05/2011
FTSE Small Cap	77	3.6	2.2	30/04/2011
FTSE All-Share	81	3.6	2.5	15/05/2011
FTSE Fledgling	51	6.4	1.2	05/05/2011
FTSE AIM All-Share	22	4.1	3.1	16/05/2011

Indices

The FTSE 100 comprises the 100 largest companies with a main listing on the London Stock Exchange. These companies are often referred to as the Blue Chips.

The FTSE 250 covers the next largest companies, often referred to as the mid caps, and the FTSE 350 includes all the companies in the FTSE 100 and FTSE 250 indices. As the names imply, there are always the same numbers of companies in these indices – if a company is taken over then it is replaced with a company from the top of the next index down.

The FTSE Small Cap Index comprises all but the smallest companies outside the FTSE 350 Index that have a full listing and is added to the FTSE 350 to form the All-Share Index.

The smallest companies, those whose stock market capitalisations are less than 0.1% of the LSE total, go into the Fledgling index. This index also contains the most illiquid stocks, that is the ones with least stock market trading in the shares.

As its name implies, the AIM All-Share index includes all companies with shares traded on the LSE's Alternative Investment Market.

Observations

Dividend payers

This column shows what proportion of companies actually pay a dividend. For example, in the FTSE 100 Index there were 92 companies paying a dividend in their most recent financial year. The percentage is notably lower even for medium-sized companies with the Small Caps slightly lower still.

It is worth noting that only just over half of the Fledglings pay a dividend and fewer than one in four of the companies on AIM reward their shareholders.

Average yield

The average yield on FTSE 100 companies was, as one would expect, the lowest at 3.3%. Surprisingly, however, the yield on Small Caps was equal to those for Mid Caps rather than a little larger. Clearly the market does not feel there is a much greater risk.

The Fledglings do offer a much higher average yield – to reward investors for the risk of holding the shares. Trading in these companies is usually quite illiquid so it may be difficult to sell shares if things go wrong.

AIM shares offer better yields than for share in the All-Share Index, again reflecting the higher risk of dividends being reduced or scrapped.

Average dividend cover

The larger the company, the more times the dividend is likely to be covered, another factor that suggests that blue chip shares are the safest investment.

Cover for Fledglings is alarmingly low at only 1.2, barely enough to cover the dividends. No wonder that yields are so high to reflect the palpable risk that dividends may have to be reduced.

AIM companies offer the best dividend cover of all – but only in the minority of cases where a dividend is paid.

Average payment date

As noted in an earlier chapter, when the dividend is actually paid tends to be something of a lottery and does not depend on the size of the company.

Key points

- Larger companies are more likely to pay dividends than smaller ones.

- Companies with a full listing are more likely to pay dividends than those on AIM.

- Those AIM companies that do pay dividends tend to have higher yields.

Chapter 13
Share Buybacks

There are sometimes situations where prospects can look superficially tempting for dividend investors but caution is required. The opposite is true of share buybacks, which at first sight seem to act against the interests of dividend investors but which should by no means be dismissed out of hand.

Companies that announce share buyback programmes can look attractive because:

1. They are making substantial profits.

2. They are generating piles of cash.

3. They have so much money piled up in reserves that the directors don't know what to do with it all.

4. The directors prefer to return cash to shareholders rather than squander it.

However, handing money to the shareholders by buying back shares is counter intuitive because:

1. It implies that the directors have run out of ideas.

2. It benefits those who sell the shares rather then those who stay loyal.

3. All shareholders are not treated equally.

The basic theory behind buying back shares is that the exercise props up, or even boosts, the share price. The board argues that the shares are undervalued and that it is buying them back on the cheap, a dubious argument and one that, if it worked, would benefit those seeking a quick profit.

In any case, one may argue that raising the dividend will do more for the share price than buying back shares.

Surprisingly, it is dividend investors, rather than those seeking capital gains, who tend to do quite well investing in companies with buyback programmes.

Companies often accompany a share buyback with an increased dividend or a special dividend so that the benefits are shared between those who want to sell and those who want to stay loyal.

With fewer shareholders, future profits – and dividends – will be divided less thinly so in theory remaining shareholders will have a greater share of the booty.

If a company in which you have invested launches a share buyback programme, ask yourself: "What's in it for me?" Your loyalty will depend on whether you feel that your interests are being given due consideration.

Case study: Domino's Pizza

Few companies can match the success story of the pizza delivery firm. Indeed, such has been the sales growth that anything less than double digit improvement came to be regarded as failure.

Once the operation was up and running with three outlets near to Milton Keynes, the business model was an ideal cash cow. Franchisees paid for the right to open new outlets under the Domino's name, so expanding the chain actually brought in revenue rather then costing the company money on buying or leasing premises. The Group was able to enjoy controlled expansion so management never got overstretched, while supplies came from a central point so quality could be maintained.

Because outlets delivered pizzas to customers' homes, there was no need to build an expensive restaurant chain or struggle to maintain standards of waiter service. Domino's was quick to embrace the internet as an effective way to boost sales.

The UK chain had reached 665 stores out of a target of 1,200 by the time results for the 2010 calendar year were announced on 15 February 2011. The figures were typical of Domino's success story: revenue up 21%; sales at outlets opened for more than a year up 11.9%; online sales 63% ahead; pre-tax profits 27% higher; and operating margins topping 20% after a decade of growth starting from 8.5%.

Chart 13.1 – Share price chart for Domino's Pizza

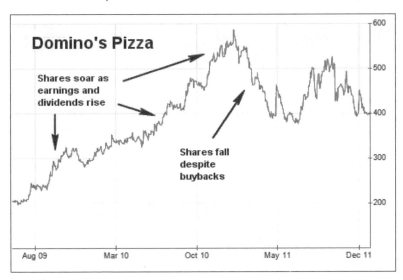

Yet the shares, already well down from a peak of 589p, fell 4% to 503p on the day of the announcement. The market took fright at news that sales in the first seven weeks of 2011 were up only 4.7%. One says "only" because, while 4.7% growth was beyond the dreams of many companies in the economic uncertainty, it was pedestrian by Domino's standards.

Domino's did raise the final dividend, a payment of 5.7p making a total of 10.2p. That gave a yield of only 2.03% at the current share price and a yield of 1.73% at the point when the shares, propelled in part by the share buyback programme, reached their peak.

A total of £4.7 million was spent buying back 1.2 million of the 162 million shares in 2010. The fall in the share price meant that further buybacks were likely. This was good news for those looking for capital gains but not much use for those wanting to buy in for an increased dividend.

Spending the buyback money on dividends equated to an extra 2.9p a share.

Table 13.1 – Financial history for Domino's Pizza

	2006	2007	2008	2009	2010
EPS (p)	6.10	8.48	10.86	13.81	17.36
Dividend (p)	3.06	4.40	5.90	7.75	10.20
Dividend cover	1.99	1.93	1.84	1.78	1.7

Source: London Stock Exchange

The prospective yield, as calculated by Morningstar financial website at 2.7%, was reasonably secure, although the dividend cover was less than 2 and had been for several years. It was admittedly not particularly attractive when the average yield of the travel and leisure sector, of which Domino's was a member, stood at 3.4% and the market at 3.7%, but the company had a good record of increasing dividends.

Fashions change

Share buybacks, like many other aspects of corporate life, tend to run in cycles. In the early 2000s it was fashionable for companies to load up with debt to buy back shares on the dubious argument that this made the balance sheet more efficient. The idea was that interest payments were cheaper than dividends.

This ludicrous notion collapsed when debt-laden companies found that, while they could reduce the dividend in hard times, there was no escape from the lenders who, when scenting blood, would ramp up the supposedly cheap interest rates and charge fees on top.

Although this fad of borrowing to buy back shares has largely disappeared, it is worth noting because it will undoubtedly re-emerge some day. Never invest for dividends in a company that borrows money to buy back shares. Its priorities are all wrong.

Thankfully the lesson does seem to have been learnt by the current generation of directors because the decision by the Bank of England to keep interest rates at 0.5% for over two years did not spark a run of cheap borrowing.

Cash is better than debt

The post-credit crunch era instead spawned a belief in hoarding cash, partly as a buffer against prolonged recession and partly in the hope that it would be possible to take over struggling companies on the cheap. When these respective fears and hopes failed to materialise, many companies found themselves awash with cash earning pitiful rates of interest.

So much cash, in fact, that some companies could afford to buy back shares *and* raise the dividend substantially. In such cases dividend investors should concentrate on the dividend increase, *not* the share buy back.

For instance, early in 2011, mining group Rio Tinto pledged to buy back over £3 billion worth of shares over two years but it also promised to raise its dividend substantially. At the same time, rival BHP Billiton added another £4 billion to its buyback programme while raising the dividend by 10%.

In such cases it is important to check the prospective yield of the company concerned before buying the shares. The extra dividend will almost certainly have been fully reflected in the share price. However, if you already own the shares you may as well stay in and enjoy the enhanced returns.

Case Study: BAT

The international tobacco giant announced plans to buy back £750 million worth of shares early in 2011 alongside strong results, yet the shares promptly fell by 16.5p to 2396.5p. So much for share buybacks propping up the share price!

Chart 13.2 – Share price chart for BAT

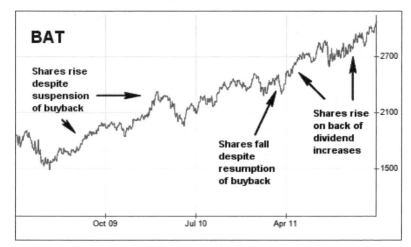

The maker of Dunhill, Lucky Strike, Pall Mall and Kent had suspended share buybacks two years earlier in the wake of the financial crisis and the resumption had been well anticipated. As such, the possibility of BAT spending cash on shares rather than dividends was a reason for dividend investors to be more cautious.

What caused the admittedly fairly modest fall in the share price was that the share buyback was to be much smaller than expected. Yet this actually made the now cheaper shares more attractive for those who wanted income rather than a return of capital.

Revenue had risen 5% to £14.9 billion in 2010 and pre-tax profits grew even faster, up 7% to £4.4 billion, boosted by higher sales in emerging markets and a 7% rise in sales of the top brands, the ones that BAT was relying on for future growth.

Chief Executive Paul Adams pointed out that emerging markets and some developed ones were showing economic growth but disposable incomes remained under pressure. What he could have said, but didn't, was that smokers seem to find the money from somewhere even when unemployed, such is the power of the addiction.

Table 13.2 – Financial history for BAT

	2006	2007	2008	2009	2010
EPS (p)	98.9	108.5	129.6	153.8	176.7
Dividend (p)	55.9	66.2	85.7	99.5	114.2
Dividend cover	1.77	1.64	1.55	1.55	1.55

Source: London Stock Exchange

BAT raised its final dividend by 13p to 81p, making a 15% increase on the total for the year, a much higher rise than the improvement in earnings. This was good news for dividend investors and the fall in the share price was a little icing on the cake.

The yield, based on the 2010 payment, was an attractive 4.3% for anyone considering buying the shares.

Ones to avoid

As a dividend investor you should most certainly not get drawn into companies that are buying back shares merely to keep the share price up after a heavy fall. This is really of no use to you. It is no substitute for generating profits and paying dividends.

Ask yourself why the shares fell so heavily in the first place:

1. Have the problems been addressed?

2. Could the money being spent on buybacks be put to better use in the company?

In an extreme case it might be better to wind the company up and divide the proceeds among all the shareholders.

Key points

- Share buybacks benefit dividend investors indirectly because future earnings will be divided among fewer shareholders.

- Buybacks imply that the company has run out of ideas for investing the money to grow profits.

- Buybacks are much more acceptable if some of the surplus cash is also paid out in increased dividends.

- Buybacks have a patchy record in propping up the share price.

Chapter 14
Flotations

We have naturally looked mainly at situations where dividend-seekers would want to invest, but they should also be aware of specific situations where they should shy away. One such scenario is share flotations. It is far better to miss the chance to get into a promising company rather than risk buying a pig in a poke.

Beware, especially, companies that have been previously bought out and delisted by private equity firms and are now returning to the stock market.

All companies coming to market are obliged to issue a prospectus giving details of the nature of the business, its financial performance, who the directors are and much more besides. This document will be lengthy and complicated so negative factors can be difficult to spot among all the information. Financial results will be 'pro forma', which means the actual results have been translated into the form they would have taken had the company been listed.

This can make them quite difficult to follow.

In particular, they may include an indication of what dividends would have been paid had the company been listed. This is purely hypothetical and should be treated with a large pinch of salt. The fact is that the company was not listed so the projection is little more than guesswork. It is most certainly *not* a cast iron guarantee of what dividends will be paid in the current year unless the prospectus specifically gives a definite figure.

If you are tempted by a new flotation, here are some points that you should bear in mind:

1. Why are the current owners selling?

2. Does the company make a profit?

3. How long has it been profitable?

4. Has the company had a previous listing and if so what has been going on since it went private?

5. What does the prospectus say about dividends?

Where the cash goes to the company

What is the money for?

1. **Clearing debt.** An admirable sentiment, especially if credit is tight or expensive, but worthwhile for the company only if your dividend is less expensive than bank interest. If this gets the company on a sounder financial footing that allows longer-term planning it is a reason to invest.

2. **Providing working capital.** Again, getting the company on a sound financial footing is a positive move.

3. **Providing resources for expanding operations.** This is the best reason for floating. The company plans to do what it knows best and sees opportunities to increase sales.

4. **Providing cash for acquisitions.** Again the business is expanding but one should be more cautious of achieving this through acquisitions rather than organic growth. With extra cash available the company may overpay for acquisitions. You need to be able to trust existing management to spend the money wisely.

Case Study: Ocado

Waitrose, the supermarket arm of John Lewis, was at the forefront of the revival in home deliveries.

The very supermarkets that destroyed the doorstep service provided by local butcher, baker and milkman some 50 years earlier spectacularly revived the arrangement, but now it was for the 'cash rich, time poor' generation rather than for busy working-class mums.

Tesco and Sainsbury's opted for their own delivery service but Waitrose had an arm's length arrangement with a specialist fleet called Ocado, which it partly owned.

Eventually, in the summer of 2010, Waitrose decided to float off Ocado, although keeping a 10.4% stake.

There were various reasons to resist any temptation to buy:

1. Ocado had never made a profit in ten years of trading.

2. There was no immediate prospect of a dividend.

3. While Ocado was free to pursue other possible clients, it was hard to see who would want a tie-in with a delivery firm so heavily linked to one customer.

4. Waitrose promised to retain Ocado as its delivery agent for the foreseeable future but there was the bizarre possibility that it would set up its own rival. In the event, it sold its remaining stake and started to compete within the M25 motorway early in 2011.

In February 2011 Ocado reported a pre-tax loss of £12.2 million for the year to 28 November.

There were some positive signs. Ocado said it had actually made a profit of £300,000 in the final three months of the financial year and the full-year loss was half that of the previous year.

Chief Executive Tim Steiner, one of the original founders of Ocado, claimed that the company had delivered on the targets set out at its flotation and that Ocado's growth was outpacing the market.

Chart 14.1 – Share price chart for Ocado

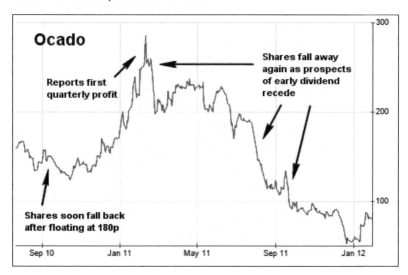

However, there was no case for dividend investors to get involved. The shares were floated at 180p and rose to 247.75p after the results, which meant the shares had been strictly for those seeking short-term capital gains.

Soon Ocado shares were slipping back to the flotation price.

Key points

- Flotations rarely offer a chance to buy into strong companies on the cheap.

- In times of financial and economic uncertainty advisers may risk bringing only second rate companies to market.

- When markets are rising strongly you will see high-quality share issues but there is a risk of being stampeded into overpaying.

- A rush of flotations may be a signal that the stock market is about to peak.

- Companies coming to market may be loaded with debt – interest payments take priority over dividends.

- Companies that were previously delisted may have changed dramatically while in private hands, not necessarily for the better from the private investor's point of view.

- Prospectuses are complicated and highly detailed so it is difficult to make an informed judgement.

- Any projections of what dividends might have been paid had the company been listed earlier are purely hypothetical. Do not rely on them as a guide to future dividends.

- Be content to let the shares settle before considering buying in. Newly floated shares often surge in the first few days after the listing only to fall back later.

Chapter 15
Turning Companies Round

Dividend investors will, on the whole, be looking for solid rather than risky investments but it can still pay to look at companies that have fared badly in the recent past if there is reason to believe that better times are arriving.

This does involve an element of risk, as it could be a false dawn. Questions to consider are:

1. Is there new management with a better grasp of the business?

2. If not, has existing management learnt from past mistakes?

3. Were the problems internal or were there external factors beyond the board's control?

4. Have trading conditions improved?

5. Are they likely to deteriorate again?

The concerns for dividend investors

These are questions for any investors to ask but for dividend investors there are additional considerations. After all, if the difficulties have put the dividend at risk we should be shying away.

We therefore need to ask further questions:

1. Has the dividend been maintained so far?

2. Has it been re-based to a lower but more sustainable level?

3. Has dividend cover slipped below 2?

4. Has the dividend been fully covered or has the company drawn on reserves?

5. Has the board made any comments on dividend policy in the light of the difficulties?

We naturally want to look at the yield. If the figure is very high, then it may be that investors fear a cut in the dividend. If the figure is very low, the shares may be overpriced. There is no hard and fast measure. We must use our own research and judgement to form an opinion. In these circumstances, it is better to err on the side of caution and walk away.

If the business is cyclical, riding up and down on the economic wave, then its nascent recovery may be based on improving conditions beyond management control, which is fine until the cycle turns down again.

Take a look at the share price. If it has recovered strongly, then the market believes that the good times are starting to roll. However, this does mean that you will now get fewer shares, and therefore fewer dividends, for your money, so you should beware of chasing after the shares. It may be better to admit that you missed the best chance to invest and look elsewhere.

If the shares are still in the doldrums, either the market has failed to spot the opportunity or other investors are sceptical. You should look at the company and what it is saying very carefully but if, at the end of the day, you believe that the company has genuinely turned the corner then be prepared to back your own judgement.

Case study: Prudential

Transformations from zero to hero take time and effort but Prudential Chief Executive Tidjane Thiam made a decent fist of it after his disastrous attempt to buy the Asian assets of fallen American insurance giant AIG.

Thiam had not been at the helm for long when he launched his "deal of a lifetime". The Pru was already well established in Asia, using cash generated in its longer standing UK and US operations to buy into the more promising oriental markets with an emerging consumer class and younger demographics.

The US financial crisis produced an interesting proposition: AIG was caught up in the debacle and was bailed out by the US Government. Selling assets was the fastest way that Washington could get its money back.

Pru offered £21.8 billion for AIA, AIG's Asian operations. It was to be paid for, in part, through a massive £14.5 billion rights issue. It was also clear that profitable Western assets would have to be sold to fund the push eastwards.

A full-scale shareholder revolt erupted at Prudential with an intensity rarely seen in the City. Given that the US Government was conducting a fire sale, it seemed that Thiam had failed to beat down the price.

As it became increasingly clear that shareholders would vote against the proposed acquisition, Thiam suffered the ignominy of having to try to renegotiate the price. A humiliating rebuff followed and when it all fell apart in June 2010, critics believed that the chief executive's position was untenable. The same could be said of Chairman Harvey McGrath, who had failed to curb Thiam's hubris.

The cost of the aborted adventure, including fees for advisers and a penalty clause for defaulting on the deal, came to £377 million, cash that could have been spent on developing the existing businesses or handed to shareholders.

Chart 15.1 – Share price chart for Prudential

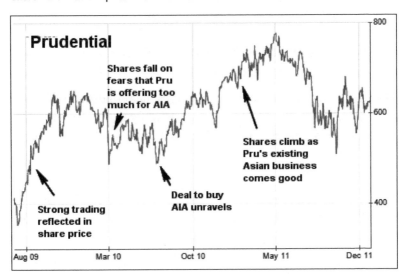

Pru shares, which had peaked at 811p in 2007, fell to a low of 489p in July 2010 just after the AIA deal was buried.

Thiam, however, was made of sterner stuff than his critics believed. So was McGrath. The following March they were able to announce impressive results for the year to 31 December 2010.

Pre-tax profits rose 33% to top £2 billion, with new business up 23% at almost £3.5 billion. Despite the failure to buy AIA, Asia accounted for £1.5 billion of the new business, which was more than either the US or the UK contributed.

The final dividend of 17.24p took the total for the year to 23.85p, an increase of 20%.

Naturally, Thiam claimed credit for the excellent 2010 results, boasting that Prudential remained the same great company it had been before the AIA debacle (though, he omitted to remark, minus £377 million).

By building on its own foundations rather than someone else's, Pru had developed its sound policy of avoiding the most competitive markets of Japan and Taiwan, concentrating instead on high-growth areas such as Malaysia.

Thiam's position looked untenable immediately after the AIA debacle. After 2010 it looked unassailable, which could be a good thing for the Pru. While he remained in charge he would hardly dare to launch any more foolhardly sorties.

While the prospect of Asian acquisitions remained, a rights issue, and certainly a large one, was off the agenda.

The results came after the share price had already recovered somewhat to top 700p but they still prompted a further jump of 35p to 749p. While the best chance to buy back in had long since gone, the shares still had their attractions.

Based on the 2010 dividend the yield was 3.2%, with the prospect of better to come. Prudential had a progressive dividend policy and with profits forecast to reach £2.2 billion in 2011 there was every prospect of a further dividend increase.

Table 15.1 – Financial history for Prudential

Prudential	2007	2008	2009	2010
Profits (£m)	1,058	- 2,074	1,564	2,072
EPS (p)	28.8	- 16.0	27.6	56.7
Dividend (p)	18.00	18.90	19.85	23.85

Source: London Stock Exchange

Restoring dividends

Why restoring a dividend is a Good Thing

Companies that restore their dividends after a period of non-payment usually look attractive because:

1. The directors will not restore the dividend unless they are confident it can be maintained.

2. The share price is likely to be depressed because investors have been scared off while the company was in difficulties.

3. Any accumulated losses that prevent the payment of a dividend will have been eliminated by recent profits or a capital restructuring.

4. The directors expect the company to continue to be profitable, otherwise a fresh wave of losses will prevent dividend payments in the foreseeable future.

However, dividends tend to be restored at a low level, certainly much lower than the level at which they were suspended. This is sensible, as it leaves open the prospect of progressively raising the dividend, but it does mean that the payout is likely to be held down for some time.

This should be reflected in the share price, so the prospective yield could be above average. As always with investing, you should make your own investigations to decide whether you are convinced that the newly restored dividend is sustainable and whether the prospective yield compensates for the risks.

The re-instatement of a dividend is obviously good news, whatever your investment aims. It is likely to result in a rise in the share price as well as providing income for shareholders.

Directors will rarely if ever re-instate a dividend unless they are very confident that they can at least maintain the initial payout and they will almost certainly err on the side of caution by pitching the dividend at a level that can be increased if things go according to plan.

No board likes to suffer the ignominy of scrapping a dividend; even more abhorrent is to repeat the process.

What shape is the company in?

As ever, it is important to look carefully at the company that is restoring its dividend before investing in it. Points to consider are:

1. Was the restoration of the dividend expected and was this already reflected in the share price?

2. Has the restoring of the dividend caused the share price to rise to an unreasonably high level?

3. What are the prospects for increasing the dividend?

4. Has new management been brought in?

5. What visibility of future earnings is there?

6. What is the outlook for the sector in which the company operates?

7. How stable are the geographic markets?

8. Have the factors that caused the dividend to be scrapped been eliminated?

We need to look not only at the prospective yield, which will give us some idea of what increases in the dividend have been factored into the share price, but also at the forward P/E, which tells us whether the current share price rating is counting on strong earnings growth.

We may decide to invest even if the share price has risen on the basis, or in anticipation of, the good news. As dividend investors, we are interested in the yield and if prospects are good then we are not particularly bothered about movements in the share price.

We have admittedly missed the best chance to get in but we can learn from this experience. Perhaps we were right not to commit ourselves to a risky investment before we were sure that the dividend would be restored, which is a perfectly reasonable line to take.

However, this is not a time to look back with regrets; what of the future?

First and foremost we want to know whether the problems that led to the suspension of the dividend have been dealt with. Were they caused by:

- lax management?
- factors outside the company's control?
- both of these?

If management was badly at fault then it is likely, although by no means necessarily the case, that those responsible have departed. If the culprits are still there, a little humility is in order. We want to be sure that they realise that they went wrong as well as being sure that they have taken measures to avoid a repeat.

Unrepentant management should be given a wide berth.

Whether or not there are new directors, we want to know:

1. What has been done to address the specific problems?

2. What changes to strategy have been made?

3. What measures, if any, have been taken to reduce costs or bring in needed expertise?

4. What attempts have been made to find new markets?

5. What new product lines have been introduced?

6. What, if anything, has been done to diversify the business?

Factors outside management's control look trickier but tend to offer us a more straightforward investment decision.

If management was able to blame freak unfavourable circumstances for the company's earlier woes then it is less likely that heads have rolled but we still need to know if any lessons have been learnt and whether evasive action has been taken to avoid a repeat.

Key questions are:

1. Could the adverse circumstances be repeated?

2. Is the company still at the mercy of these events?

3. Has the company diversified to reduce the impact?

While mistakes of management can be avoided in future, events outside the company's control are highly likely to recur and in this sense our investment decision is much more clear cut.

Unless we can be really sure that the past has been consigned to history it is safer to stay well clear.

Case study: St Modwen

Property group St Modwen answered the prayers of its shareholders when it restored its dividend for the year to November 2010 after passing just one year's payout. Given the collapse of the property market in the aftermath of the credit crunch and ensuing recession, this was a much shorter gap than one might have expected.

St Modwen had enjoyed a progressive dividend policy until the end of 2008, raising its payout from 6.07p to 10.8p over a five-year period but the warning signs were already there when the 2008 dividend had to be paid entirely out of reserves as the Group ran up a loss.

Table 15.2 – Financial history for St Modwen

	2003	2004	2005	2006	2007	2008	2009	2010
EPS	14.6p	13.1p	51.1p	56.7p	14.3p	-39.6p	-59.7p	18.6p
Dividend	6.07p	6.99p	7.36p	8.56p	9.84p	10.8p	-	3p
Cover	2.41	1.87	6.95	6.62	1.45	-	-	6.2

Source: Morningstar Premium

We can see that dividend cover varied widely from year to year but St Modwen sensibly resisted the temptation to raise the payout too quickly, given the vicissitudes of the property market, and this policy enabled the payment of a dividend in 2008 even though the Group ran up a loss that year.

However, when losses continued to mount, St Modwen wisely scrapped the interim and then the final dividend in 2009.

On the way down the shares lost over 90% of their value. Given the well-publicised problems of the property and building sector, dividend investors needed to consider quite early on whether it was better to sell up despite the progressive dividend and look for a safer haven.

Chart 15.2 – Share price chart for St Modwen

St Modwen shares started their decline a little earlier than the stock market as a whole. Those who missed the warning signs did have an opportunity to get out in 2008 when the shares temporarily surged to just below 500p.

So much for history. What of the future?

St Modwen paid an interim dividend of 1p, announced with half-year results in July 2010, and a final 2p along with full-year results in February 2011.

The good news for dividend investors was that the restoration of the dividend was not greeted by a sharp recovery in the share price. After a pick-up from 60p to 250p in 2009, as shorter-term traders capitalised on the view that the fall had been overdone, the shares drifted again, to settle around 175p.

Thus dividend investors who were understandably cautious when the interim dividend was restored still had the opportunity to buy with a yield of 1.7% based on the 2010 dividend. House broker Numis Securities was forecasting an increased dividend of 3.5p, giving a prospective yield of 2%, while the market as a whole was yielding nearly twice that.

Points in favour

1. St Modwen had acted sensibly in its dividend policy and had restored the payout at a level that could be increased year by year. The dividend cover for 2010 was a whopping six times.

2. The Group had carved out a niche re-generating properties in regional markets where cheaper land offset lower returns compared with prime property markets in city centres. Working on brownfield sites such as the former MG Rover plant at Longbridge was politically popular and planning permission was easier and quicker to obtain.

3. St Modwen had a strong balance sheet and a landbank of 5,700 acres that Chief Executive Bill Oliver described as "full of latent value". He added that the development pipeline was strengthening and a number of significant schemes were being put together.

4. Gearing had been reduced from 80% to 72%, admittedly a small reduction but one that would help to offset the effect of rising interest rates.

5. The long-term development programme was underpinned by a rental income stream from a portfolio of properties. The rent roll increased 5% in 2010 with empty space reduced from 17% to 12%.

6. If you wanted a property or building company in your portfolio St Modwen was better than most players in a battered sector.

Points against

1. However the figures were dressed up, there was no getting away from the fact that the yield was quite low. There were much better yielding shares elsewhere.

2. With the shares showing no signs of recovery it was possible that a better chance to buy in would present itself further down the line.

3. Shareholders were entitled to ask why things had gone so badly wrong in 2008 and 2009 if the business model was so impressive.

4. There was still a long way to go before the dividend would get back to where it was before it was scrapped.

St Modwen was back on the right track and was no longer one for dividend investors to avoid. However, the comparatively low yield meant that it was one for those prepared to take a gamble on the longer term and was still unsuitable for those wanting income immediately.

Those investors who had held onto their shares through the dividend suspension would probably want to hold on and enjoy the better times; the case for buying in was less compelling.

Case study: ITV

The competitive pressures in the broadcasting industry took a heavy toll on Britain's first commercial TV station. Just as ITV had, 50 years earlier, wooed away audiences from the BBC with lavish spending, so had ITV been battered and outspent by BSkyB.

The BBC's response back in the 1960s was to launch a second channel, which increased costs without necessarily adding to the total number of viewers. ITV has likewise added channels which increase costs without adding greatly to the amount of advertising spend.

ITV reduced its dividend in 2008 and scrapped it in 2009 but the shares were sliding well before these blows as the channel struggled.

Table 15.3 – Financial history for ITV

ITV	2006	2007	2008	2009	2010
EPS (p)	5.4	5.0	1.8	1.8	6.4
Dividend (p)	3.15	3.15	0.68	Nil	Nil
Dividend cover	1.71	1.59	2.67	NA	NA

Source: London Stock Exchange

Profits for 2010 were boosted by the football World Cup held in South Africa in the summer, despite the fact that only England of the home nations managed to qualify and the team's performance left much to be desired.

The encouraging news extended into 2011 with advertising revenue in the first quarter rising 8% compared with the start of 2010. The wedding of Prince William and Kate Middleton provided a further boost to advertising, partly because the event would attract a large television audience and partly because the extra day's bank holiday would boost the number of republican DIY enthusiasts and leisure seekers that day.

Furthermore, ITV seemed to have got its act together after several years of losing viewers, not only to satellite channels but also to the BBC. Love them or hate them, *The X Factor, I'm a Celebrity* and *Dancing on Ice* were crowd pleasers.

However, a recovery in the share price 2009 and 2010 was overdone and the shares started to drift again.

Chart 15.3 – Share price chart for ITV

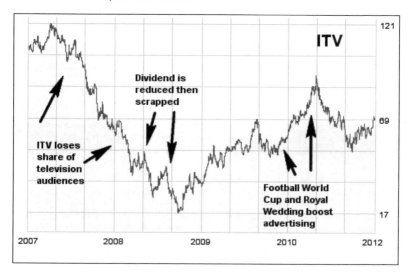

One of the advantages of ITV from the investor's point of view is that there is some visibility of earnings. Advertising is booked in advance so you have quite a clear idea of what revenue will be for the next four or five months. This is in sharp contrast to retailing, where we have to work with sales figures over the previous few weeks.

One reason why ITV scrapped its dividend was that it was struggling with a high burden of debt. The company had learnt its lesson and was repaying borrowings so quickly that analysts expected it to clear the debt by the end of 2011. That meant cash for dividends would no longer be siphoned off in interest payments.

Reasons for investing in ITV early in 2011 were:

1. Advertising revenue was rising.

2. Forecasts were for a 3% increasing in revenue for 2011.

3. Debt was being cleared.

4. The share price had not risen far.

Reasons for not investing:

1. The Royal Wedding was a one-off event.

2. The World Cup would not be repeated in 2011.

3. Advertising could fall away again if consumers cut back spending as they were squeezed by frozen wage rates, rising interest rates and higher taxes.

4. There was wide ranging competition for advertising, not only from other televisions channels but from radio, newspapers and magazine, junk mail, websites and posters.

With hindsight we can now see that the Royal Wedding was a huge success, helping to push spending on television advertising up a remarkable 18% after a 7-8% year-on-year rise in the first quarter.

However, this was no reason to pile into ITV shares because:

1. This increase was spread across all commercial TV channels and was not going just to ITV.

2. ITV itself had not retracted its earlier warning that the state of the economy made it difficult to predict advertising spend over the whole year.

3. The economy showed little or no growth over the six months to the end of March 2011.

4. The rise in TV advertising was patchy, with growth of only 6% and 3% in January and March respectively interspersed by 13% in February.

5. The Government was cutting its advertising budget, some of which is allocated to TV.

Dividend investors needed to consider whether there was any reasonable hope not only that the dividend would be restored but that a progressive dividend policy would be possible. There were just too many doubts hanging over ITV, whose dividend had gone in the wrong direction over the previous five years.

The reduction of advertising spend during the economic downturn and the intense competition from different forms of media would severely hamper ITV in its recovery. It was likely that management would want to rebuild reserves and pay down debt rather than risk restoring an unsustainable dividend. Having suffered the ignominy of first reducing and then scrapping the dividend, the board would err on the side of caution.

With so many concerns it is best to look for safer havens rather than gamble on buying the shares cheaply in the hope of picking up a large number of shares and enjoying future dividends.

Key points

- Determine why the company got into difficulties and whether those issues have been dealt with.

- Assess the ability of existing management to turn the company round.

- Accept that turnarounds carry higher risks but offer potentially greater rewards.

- Consider whether the recovery is fully reflected in the share price.

- Companies rarely restore the dividend unless they are sure they can maintain it.

- Restored dividends often turn into progressive dividends.

- The shares may remain relatively cheap for some time as investors who sold when the dividend was scrapped will remain wary of buying back in.

Chapter 16
Rights Issues and Placings

If we should be suspicious of buybacks, we should be horrified at rights issues, where companies offer existing shareholders the right to buy more shares.

This is bad news because:

1. We want the company to be handing money to us, not the other way round.

2. We may not have spare cash at that particular moment.

3. If we wanted to buy more shares in the company we would have done so on the stock market, deciding for ourselves how many to buy.

4. The share price will almost always fall, making it less attractive to sell out and invest elsewhere.

5. The company may have to pay underwriters to subscribe for any shares that are not taken up by the existing shareholders.

6. The company will certainly have to pay advisers and the fees can swallow a substantial proportion of the money raised.

Alas, rights issues often come out of the blue, in which case you have no chance of getting out ahead of the event. Warning signs are if the company:

- is burning cash and will run out of money in the foreseeable future

- has heavy debts which it may choose to reduce by issuing equity

- is in danger of breaching its banking covenants

- is seeking to expand aggressively through acquisitions

- is growing rapidly organically and stretching resources

- is the subject of press speculation that it will make a rights issue.

All these potential issues will be thrown up if we research companies before we invest and keep in touch with developments subsequently. Nor does it necessarily involve detailed and time-consuming research. We should not be investing in companies burning cash in the first place and we should be very wary of companies with large debts.

Nonetheless, despite all our best endeavours we may still be hit with a rights issue that we did not see coming and in such cases it is generally best to take up your rights in full because:

1. The rights shares will normally be priced below the prevailing stock market price and may possibly be at a substantial discount.

2. If we do not apply for our entitlement we will see our holding diluted by new shares taken up by other shareholders.

3. If we do buy the shares we can always sell part or all of our holding after we receive our allotment.

Two notes of caution:

1. It is unusual for one rights issue to be followed by a second one but it can happen. Assess whether the money raised is enough to deal with the company's cash shortfall, and read any comment in the press. If you fear that more money will be needed, take your rights this time and sell out as soon as possible.

2. If the stock market price falls below the rights issue price then do *not* take up your rights. Not only is it pointless to pay a higher price, but this is a warning signal that there are deep-seated problems. You should consider selling in the market in these circumstances.

Placings

A company you have invested in may choose to raise cash by placing shares with institutional investors rather then make a rights issue.

Although this does not benefit you directly, it is arguably more palatable for existing dividend shareholders because:

1. Existing shareholders do not have to stump up any cash.

2. The new investors will normally be offered only a tiny discount to the stock market price so they are not getting in on the cheap.

3. The share price will probably not fall heavily if it is known that new investors are willing to come in near to the current price level.

4. The new investors are giving the company a vote of confidence.

5. A wider shareholder base means the shares become more liquid, making it easier for us to sell on the stock market should we subsequently wish to do so.

These points are admittedly of more interest to those looking to sell rather than for dividend investors, but even the longest term holders occasionally need to assess whether to cut and run.

It is true that existing shareholders will have their holdings diluted and the dividend pot will have to be spread more thinly. However, the extra cash will, one hopes, generate higher earnings per share, either by being used to boost the business or by reducing the burden of interest payments on loans.

Claw backs

Placings are sometimes accompanied by an 'open offer' to allow existing shareholders to subscribe for new shares. This gives you the right to claw back some of the placing shares and thus avoid having your holding diluted.

You will pay the same price per share as the new investors. This arrangement has the merit of allowing you to increase your stake if you wish to do so or to stand back if you are fully invested. Do your homework just as you would if you were buying into the company for the first time.

Case study: Stobart

Spotting Eddie Stobart trucks on long motorway journeys was once a way of keeping children amused. On a more serious note, what was once a Cumbrian-based family firm expanded into a formidable international haulage company with turnover now topping £500 million a year.

It has also been a dividend payer, although cover dropped below 2 from the year to 28 February 2009 onwards.

Stobart was inevitably affected by the heavy snowfall in December 2010, incurring costs of £1.5 million as a result, but a trading statement covering the three months from October to January, which included all the bad weather, showed the Group's performance to be 'significantly ahead' of the same period a year earlier.

Three months after this reassurance and somewhat out of the blue, Stobart announced a placing and open offer to raise £120 million gross, or £114.9 million after expenses (which, incidentally, is a reminder that raising money is an expensive business).

Rather unusually, this placing was at a premium to the prevailing stock market share price of 148p, which meant it would be highly unattractive to existing shareholders unless this vote of confidence on the part of new shareholders prompted the share price to rise sharply.

Table 16.1 – Financial history for Stobart

	2007-8	2008-9	2009-10	2010-11
Pre-tax profit (£m)	3.52	22.14	33.29	29.47
EPS (p)	2.1	7.7	10.8	9.7
Dividend (p)	8	6	6	6
Dividend cover	0.26	1.28	1.80	1.62

Source: London Stock Exchange

The new shares would not qualify for the 4p final dividend for 2010-11, which was perfectly reasonable since Stobart was already nearly two months into its next financial year, but this was an added drawback for dividend investors.

Chart 16.1 – Share price chart for Stobart

In the event, the share price fell to 125p as a proposed acquisition, to be funded by the new cash, provoked controversy. The plan was to buy a portfolio of property from William Stobart, grandson of the founder, and Andrew Tinkler, Stobart's chief executive. Both were major shareholders in Stobart, owning 14.5% between them.

This was a clear cut decision for shareholders: there was absolutely no attraction for them in the rights issue. Even Tinkler and William Stobart passed up their entitlements! Yet a handful of shareholders unthinkingly applied for their rights shares.

Some people just sign up for whatever drops through the letterbox. No wonder they lose money.

Key points

- Watch for warning signs that any company you have invested in may need to raise cash and sell out if you are worried.

- You may not like rights issues but assuming you have the cash it is usually right to take up your entitlement provided the rights price is below the stock market price.

- Do not touch any rights issue with a bargepole if the stock market price falls below the rights issue price.

Chapter 17

Takeovers

Takeovers always present tricky decisions for investors, whatever their original motives for buying the shares. On the positive side:

1. You will almost always be offered a premium value for your shares.

2. Most offers are in cash or have a cash alternative so you can take your money and choose another investment.

3. If the company you invested in had failed to live up to your expectations you are rescued from your misjudgement.

4. Share prices go up after bid approaches so you have the opportunity to get out immediately rather than await the outcome of the battle.

5. Even if the bid fails, the shares may not fall all the way back to their previous level so the value of your shares has increased (although this is not particularly important for dividend investors).

6. If the share price goes back to its previous level you are no worse off than when you started.

7. At the very least, the bid prompts you to reassess your holding.

However, assuming the bid succeeds:

1. You may be offered shares in the bidding company that you possibly find unattractive.

2. You have lost the option of continuing to invest in a company that you found attractive.

3. You may incur capital gains tax.

The most important thing to remember is not to act in haste. Ignore the advice you get from either side. They are talking their own corner. You are equally entitled to decide on the action that suits you best. They are *your* shares bought with *your* money.

You must face reality

However passive an investor you are, and however long term your outlook is, takeovers are one situation where you really *must* follow developments day by day. You will probably have an opportunity to enhance your portfolio.

Your first consideration is whether, had the bid not emerged, you would have been happy to carry on leaving your investment undisturbed. Factors are similar to the ones that applied when you bought the shares:

1. Is the company increasing its profits year by year?

2. Is it raising the dividend year by year?

3. Are dividends well covered by earnings?

4. Are any interest payments well covered?

5. Is there continuity of management, so the good work so far will not be compromised by changes at the top?

6. Was there an attractive yield before the bid drove up the share price?

If the answers are all yes, then you should hang on and do nothing, at least in the initial stages of the bid. Your investment is fine as it is, you do not want to find another company to invest in and you will be quite happy if life goes back to how it was before this rude interruption.

If, however, a re-assessment of the company throws up any doubts, then you need to consider your strategy as the bid unfolds. If your answers to the questions above are mainly no, then you now have the opportunity to get out while the going is good.

Let us look at sensible options:

Sell in the market immediately after an offer is announced

You get your cash quickly without having to wait for the outcome of the bid and you are free to invest in another company with a decent yield.

This works well if:

- you were thinking of selling anyway
- you find a better investment
- no higher bid is forthcoming
- the share price on the stock market is higher than the only bid to be put forward.

It works badly if:

- a better bid comes along
- the bid fails and you have forfeited an excellent yield from the target company.

Accept the offer immediately

This works well if:

- the bid goes through quickly
- no other offer is forthcoming
- the offer on the table is generous
- the offer is in cash or in shares of a company you regard as a sound investment.

It works badly if:

- you help to push acceptances to a sufficiently high level to discourage another bidder from offering more

- another higher bid emerges and you are unable to signal your support for the better offer
- it takes ages for the bid to go through and you are unable to sell in the market and reinvest quickly.

It should be noted that, while there is little point in accepting a bid until you see how the land lies, accepting the first offer immediately is not a dire mistake. If a higher bid succeeds you will be released from your acceptance and allowed to take the better terms irrespective of whether they are offered by the original bidder or a new one.

Hold on to see what develops

This works well if:

- a higher bid emerges
- the bid fails but you retain your holding in a high yielding company.

It works badly if:

- you actually want to sell your holding but the bid fails and the share price falls.

Hold on until the share prices rises as high as you think it will go, then sell in the market

This works well if:

- you catch the top of the market – or at least get pretty close
- the bid fails after you have sold and the shares fall back.

It works badly if:

- the shares continue to rise after you have sold
- a higher bid emerges.

When the bid goes unconditional

Bids will have one or more conditions attached. At the very least, they will depend on the bidder receiving acceptances that take its holding above 50%.

Most conditions fall by the wayside fairly quickly – for instance the bid may be conditional on due diligence or on the target company's directors recommending acceptance of the offer, matters that tend to be dealt with early on. If these issues are potential stumbling blocks then the bidder will be reluctant to throw more time and money into a bid that stands a fair chance of failing.

The most important condition is the level of acceptances. Once an offer is deemed to be 'unconditional as to acceptances' then it is very, very unlikely to be dropped for some other reason. An offer that goes 'wholly unconditional' cannot subsequently be withdrawn.

Until this point you should have been reluctant to accept any offer as you wanted to keep your options open. Now, however, is the time to act. You can:

1. **Sell in the market** and get cash immediately. The price we get in the market is likely to be a little lower than the offer, reflecting the fact that we have use of our money while those accepting the bid have to wait for pay day.

2. **Accept the offer** immediately. You get the full offer price but you have to wait for up to two weeks until the cheque arrives. Given the short time span that the Takeover Code allows between the bid going unconditional and payment for your shares, you might as well hang on for the full amount.

3. **Do nothing.** This is not a sensible option. You will not get any more dividends and you will not even get cash for your holdings unless the bidder puts you out of your misery by compulsorily buying out the minority shareholders, which it is entitled to do if acceptances top 90%. You will go to the end of the queue behind all those shareholders who accepted voluntarily.

Is the bid in cash or shares?

Bids may be paid for in cash, in shares in the bidding company or as a combination of the two. Normally we would prefer cash unless the shares in the bidding company offer a good yield.

If the offer is in shares then we will be more inclined to sell in the market. Cash gives us the choice of our next investment; shares mean we are stuck with what we get.

The offer may be priced in shares in the bidding company with a cash alternative. The cash alternative may be set at a lower level than the nominal value of the shares and we must therefore decide whether to take shares or cash. In this case we are probably better off taking the shares and then, if we really wanted the cash, selling the shares in the market.

You may receive a mix-and-match offer, part in shares and part in cash, with the opportunity of asking for a higher proportion in shares or more in cash.

Your decision on whether to take shares or cash will depend on whether the bidding company offers good dividend prospects.

Case study: BSkyB

Media mogul Rupert Murdoch launched the Sky satellite TV service back in the late 1980s in direct competition with rival channel BSB. Both companies lost money in developing expensive technology while it took time to persuade the public to subscribe for the infant services.

Reality soon prevailed and the rivals came together in what was ostensibly a merger. Murdoch had the deeper pockets and the emerging BSkyB effectively came under his control.

Table 17.1 – Financial history for BSkyB

	2006-7	2007-8	2008-9	2009-10	2010-11
EPS (p)	26.3	25.1	25.9	32.1	41.6
Dividend (p)	15.5	16.75	17.6	19.4	23.28
Dividend cover	1.70	1.50	1.47	1.65	1.79

Source: London Stock Exchange

In the middle of 2010, Murdoch's News Corp, which at that stage owned 39% of BSkyB, approached the independent directors with a suggestion that Murdoch buy out the remaining 61% at 700p a share.

This was turned down with the retort that any bid would have to top 800p and the shares subsequently rose above 700p in anticipation.

Chart 17.1 – Share price chart for BSkyB

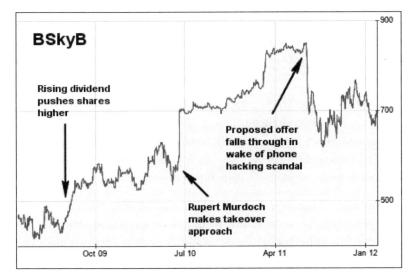

From the days when Murdoch was pumping millions of pounds into Sky, and nearly going broke in the process, the satellite broadcaster had developed into a highly successful operation with growing numbers of subscribers. It generated cash and was highly attractive to dividend investors.

Would the bid be referred?

The first consideration for shareholders was whether the bid was likely to be referred to the Competition Commission, which would delay any offer for six months. With his control of four national newspapers and a satellite TV station, Murdoch obviously had enormous power.

This was not a big worry for dividend investors, who would continue to enjoy growing dividends and who would be perfectly happy if the bid was blocked. However, it was sensible to work on the assumption that the bid would eventually be waived through on the basis that it would take a brave government minister to risk Murdoch's wrath.

Could former Labour leader Tony Blair have won three elections by a mile without the support of Murdoch newspapers? Could David Cameron have scraped enough Conservative seats to form a coalition?

The Office of Fair Trading recommended a competition inquiry but when the poisoned chalice was picked up in the following March by Culture Minister Jeremy Hunt he was able to persuade himself that the deal could go ahead after Murdoch promised to put the Sky News operation into a separate, independent company.

Interestingly, Murdoch seemed able to decide who ran BSkyB with only 39% of the shares. He would have the same stake in the 'independent' Sky News which would depend for its revenue, and survival, on a BSkyB 100% Murdoch-owned.

Editorial independence was not, however, the prime concern of shareholders. They had moved on to the next question, which was how keen Murdoch was to prevail.

Very keen. He had already tried to put together a link-up with ITV which had fallen foul of competition rules. BSkyB represented his best, probably only, chance of increasing his presence in UK television.

How much was Murdoch likely to pay?

The independent directors originally indicated that they would support nothing less than 800p a share and as part of their strategic plan they bought shares at 772p. In January 2011 BSkyB had announced record profits and one major shareholder called for 950p.

Figures for the second half of the 2010 calendar year, released just before Hunt made his fateful decision, showed a 26% rise in pre-tax profits to £467 million, boosted by buoyant demand for broadband and high-definition television (HDTV). Net debt was slashed by 44% to £945 million.

BSkyB added 140,000 subscribers in the final three months of 2010, taking its total to more than ten million.

The real icing on the cake for dividend investors was an 11% rise in the interim dividend – BSkyB's financial year runs to the end of June.

So with BSkyB shares at around 823p after Hunt signalled his consent, subject to a short consultation period, it was undoubtedly right to hold on.

Key points

- Do not put your head in the sand – study the facts and make an informed decision.

- Do not rush to accept any takeover bid – wait to see what develops.

- It is generally better to hold on rather than sell hastily in the market.

- Once a bid goes wholly unconditional, accept immediately.

Chapter 18
Ethical Investing

Although the basic idea of investing is to make money, many investors are concerned about the ethical implications of their choices. They do not wish to be seen to be supporting arms manufacturing to shore up dictators, or the sale of cigarettes to impoverished Third World nationals.

Nuclear power and drugs tested on animals produce similar horror responses.

By all means follow your conscience if you wish to. That is your prerogative. Do bear in mind that there is a price to pay for this sacrifice. At the very least you narrow down your choice of companies and possibly rule out some good dividend payers.

A definition of what constitutes ethical or unethical investments varies from person to person but the best measure is probably the FTSE4Good Index which comprises ethical companies and excludes those deemed to be beyond the pale.

According to Financial Express, a firm of independent statisticians, members of the FTSE 100, which included the likes of arms maker BAE, alcohol producers Diageo and SABMiller, and tobacco giants BAT and Imps, produced total returns of 22% over the five years to the end of 2010 compared with 3% from companies in the FTSE4Good Index.

The implications for dividend investors are particularly serious. Share prices ended the period little changed from where they started. The main gains came from dividends.

Why 'unethical' shares may be cheap

When sufficient numbers of investors shun a particular company it has the effect of holding the share price down and thereby exaggerating the yield, so unethical companies can be especially attractive for the dividend investor.

Trustees of company pension funds are required by financial regulators to consider ethical investments as part of their annual review. While most probably do little more than go through the motions, there is pressure to avoid companies seen as the worst offenders.

The first unit trust with ethical investments was Stewardship, launched by Friends Provident in the 1980s. Although it was greeted with derision at the time, it has been followed by other similar ethical funds.

Thus at the start of 2011 the sinners were sitting on prospective yields above 4% and as high as 5.5%, with dividends well covered by earnings from cash-generative businesses, while the market average was around 3.5%.

Green companies

On a more positive note, one may wish to put at least part of our investment into green companies as a passing fad. Formerly seen as 'bearded weirdos', eco-warriors have captured the mainstream of politics. There is no doubt that companies will have to pay greater attention to avoiding polluting the planet or burning up depleted resources.

One of the main problems with green investments is that the sector is moving so quickly. Technology for industries such as solar and wind power, marine energy, waste disposal and green transport is constantly being updated. As a general rule you should be looking to invest in the latest technology and not in yesterday's great idea that has been overtaken.

The dangers are:

1. Not all technology works, so money can be wasted on research that leads down a blind alley.

2. You may find yourself investing in companies before they have a proven track record or a viable product.

3. You risk having to wait years for a dividend.

4. You may be called on to make an additional investment through a rights issue.

5. Solid companies paying a solid dividend may fail to move with the times and eventually suffer from dwindling revenue.

To get a real flavour of green investing you should read *The Green Investment Handbook*.[3]

Key points

- You narrow your options if you rule out swathes of companies.

- Returns from ethical stocks may be lower than from sinners.

- In the end it is your choice.

---

[3] *The Green Investment Handbook* by Nick Hanna (Harriman House).

Chapter 19
Company Perks

The icing on the cake is temptingly delicious, all sugary and sweet – but would you buy a cake just for the icing? What about the cake itself?

This is the attitude that investors should take when they consider putting their money into the wide range of companies that offer extra perks over and above the dividend that they pay.

Shareholder perks range from tea and sandwiches at the Annual General Meeting to knocking thousands of pounds off a house purchase. The icing on the cake can be spread thinly or quite thickly.

There are two main reasons for holding shares:

1. You are looking for income from dividends.

2. You hope to sell the shares at a higher price than you paid for them.

Perks give you a third potential benefit, the icing on the cake. They are the equivalent of an extra dividend, one that can often be as large as you choose to make it.

But there is the rub. Most perks are a discount on the company's products. You end up spending more than you get back in return. Dividends and capital gains come your way without you having to shell out more money on top of the original share purchase.

Wide range of goodies

Although only about 50 of the 2,000 companies whose shares are traded on the London Stock Exchange offer shareholders discounts off their products, the goodies range from jewellery, clothing, food and drink to air fares, new and used cars, and magazines.

These perks can look very attractive but there are several disadvantages. Most obviously, if you do not want to travel by car to France or acquire a new home from a particular builder then such a concession is of no use to you. There is no point in buying shares at Moss Bros if you choose your suits at Marks & Spencer.

A minimum shareholding is often required to qualify for the perk. Although in some companies just one share is sufficient, others reserve the benefit for holders of at least 2,500 shares.

Companies may require investors to hold the shares for a minimum period, usually one year but sometimes longer.

Perks can be withdrawn or changed so it is difficult to keep track of what is currently available. Some companies notify the shareholders what perks are offered in the annual report so you may have to buy the shares first and find out your entitlement later.

Advantages of perks

1. You get something extra from your investment.

2. Companies offering perks cover a broad range of sectors so there is something for everyone.

Disadvantages of perks

1. Only a minority of companies offer perks and you may not want to invest in some or indeed any of them.

2. The perks are of no value to you if you do not want what is on offer. When you are paid cash in a dividend you can spend the money as you please. With perks you are stuck with what you are given.

3. Even where the perks are attractive the cost of buying the shares is likely to far outweigh the value of the perks. The value of your shares may go down while you hold them.

4. Perks are usually a discount on the purchase of the company's products so you have to pay out more cash on top of the original share purchase to earn them.

5. You may be required to buy a minimum number of shares or hold them for a minimum length of time to qualify.

6. You may be distracted from investing in companies that do not offer perks but which do offer better prospects of dividends and/or capital gains.

7. Perks can be changed or withdrawn at short notice at the discretion of the company's directors.

8. You will need to check with the company or its registrar whether perks are still available.

Table 19.1 shows a selection of perks that have been available, but investors will need to check with individual companies to ensure that the concessions still exist.

Table 19.1 – Sample of companies offering perks to shareholders

Company	Sector	Perk	Min. holding
Arena Leisure	Leisure	Half-price entry to racecourses	2,000 shares
Beales	Retail	10% discount on purchases of up to £5,000	2,500 shares
Bloomsbury	Publisher	35% off retail price of books	250 shares
Legal & General	Insurance	Up to 25% discount on insurance	No minimum

While it is generally not a great idea to chase after a company's shares for the perks alone, you should not scorn an investment just because you do not want the goodies on offer. If a company is making good profits and offers a decent, well-covered dividend, it is still a sound investment.

When calculating the cost of buying shares to see if a perk is worthwhile you must include your brokers' fees and the 0.5% stamp duty on all share purchases. Bear in mind that if you take your perk and then sell, you will incur selling costs, although not stamp duty, on sales.

This need not be too onerous a burden as online brokers will carry out single trades for typically £10-12, but if your perk is of low monetary value the benefit can be effectively wiped out.

Nominee accounts

Most online traders will put your shares in a nominee account, that is your holdings are lumped together with those of other online investors in one large account. This saves the cost of setting up a separate account just for you.

This is no cause for alarm: you genuinely own the shares you bought and you will receive dividends paid. You should also receive the perks. For example, Barclays Stockbrokers will claim the entitlement for you as long as your shares are held in its MarketMaster, PensionMaster or Investment ISA, although you have to ring Barclays to stake your claim.

Some companies insist, however, that shares are registered in your own name to qualify for perks, which means your broker will have to set up your own account at extra cost. These include Barratt Developments, British Land, BT and Eurotunnel. Check with your broker before you buy whether you will receive the perks.

In assessing various perks available below. I have based calculations on share prices at the end of January 2011. Share prices will change over time but the general principles remain the same.

Perks overview

Retail heaven

The sector offering most shareholder perks is undoubtedly retailing, where a wide range of companies offer discounts on their goods. These perks are generally more attractive than most because we all shop at some time and many well-known High Street names offer discounts on their goods.

These include:

Mothercare: You receive a 10% discount on up to £500 of merchandise in Mothercare and Early Learning Centres, which means you save £50. This also applies if you order by telephone or online.

However, you need to buy at least 500 shares, which will set you back £2,600. Most of us buy for somebody's children, especially at Christmas, but we may baulk at splashing out so much cash if they are not our own.

It must also be said that if you bought Mothercare shares early in 2010 you were nursing a loss of £1 a share a year later, so at that point your £50 discount had cost £500! You would also have received dividends of 16.8p a share, or £84, giving a total loss on your outlay, assuming you made full use of the discount, of about £360.

In fairness, Mothercare shares did particularly well the previous year but this does demonstrate the importance of considering any share purchase from an overall investment perspective. Last year you would actually have done better to pay full price at Mothercare and put your money in a savings account paying a pitiful rate of interest.

Marks & Spencer: Vouchers for stores and for Café Revive are sent out each year. The amount depends on the board so you are not sure what you are getting year by year and it is hard to evaluate the offer.

Moss Bros: A 20% discount voucher is sent out each year. This is a bigger discount than most retailers offer but how many suits do you buy at a time?

Next: Here the discount is a generous 25% but only on one purchase made in the summer months and you must have bought 500 shares before the end of March to qualify. The investment would set you back more than £10,000.

This was a great investment in 2009, when a purchase at around £12 a share early enough to qualify produced a gain of more than 60% by the time your voucher was due to expire. Last year also produced a capital gain, although not such a dramatic one. And in both years there were dividends on top.

The point is, however, that you did far better out of the actual investment than from the perk's discount.

Signet: There is no minimum shareholding required by this jewellery group and you get a 10% discount in H Samuel, Ernest Jones and Leslie Davis, so the reward for a modest outlay is potentially quite substantial.

Mulberry: You need 500 shares to qualify for a 20% discount card that is valid in standalone Mulberry stores but not in concessions in other stores. The shares did spectacularly well last year so a £1,000 punt at the start of 2010 was worth well over £6,000 by year end.

But therein lies the rub. New investors now need to shell out about £6,600 to earn the discount.

Thorntons: With just 200 shares you receive £34 worth of vouchers knocking 20-25% off chocolates normally costing a total of £140. At least with this one you know exactly what you are getting and many people spend that amount on choccies for themselves or other people over a year.

Thorntons' shares have performed erratically over the past few years but for an investment of under £200 those chocolates look more tempting than most goodies that companies offer. Thorntons has also paid a dividend of more than 6p a share for the past eight years and is expected to continue to do so for at least the next two.

Bricks and mortar

In contrast to retailers, where you can usually control how many items you buy at a discount and can limit your spending, some perks involve making expensive purchases – although with correspondingly larger benefits.

Such perks are found particularly in house builders such as:

Barratt Developments: Shareholders qualify for a £500 discount on every £25,000, or part of £25,000, spent on a new Barratt home in the UK or the US. So if you pay £176,000 for an average Barratt house you get £4,000 knocked off, a decent saving.

Clearly this is likely to be a one-off benefit unless you are trading up from one Barratt home to another every few years. One major pitfall is that you must hold 1,000 shares for 12 months before you make your purchase. Few people plan a house move so far in advance and you could get a job in an area where there is no Barratt building site, although they are quite widely spread.

In common with other companies in the construction sector, Barratt shares took a battering in 2007 and the first half of 2008. A recovery in 2009 petered out so those who have held the shares over the past year have lost money. Barratt has not paid a dividend since the financial year ending 30 June 2008 and, as it has reported pre-tax losses in the past two years, is not expected to pay a dividend in the current or following year.

You could take the view that with Barratt shares struggling to reach 100p the minimum outlay of less than £1,000 provides opportunity for the recovery in the housing market and therefore a rebound in Barratt shares, but that is a long-term investment decision that you should think about carefully.

Persimmon: Much of the argument that appertained to Barratt also applies to rival Persimmon, where again the minimum holding is 1,000 shares held for at least a year. However, the terms of the perk for a Persimmon or Charles Church house are less favourable.

The 2% discount is at a similar level but the maximum allowed is £4,000, however expensive the home, which must be bought in your own name. No helping out the children or grandchildren, then.

If the property is subject to special sales incentives or a price reduction you cannot claim the discount on top. In these days of sluggish housing sales, a non-shareholder who haggles is likely to be treated the same as a shareholder.

Bellway: This house builder knocks £625 off every £25,000 spent but you need 2,000 shares for at least a year. Although the discount is slightly more generous than at Barratt you need to spend about £13,000 on shares to qualify, a lot of money to tie up for 12 months.

As with Persimmon, you have to tell the sales negotiator you are claiming the discount when you reserve your house but that raises the question of whether in today's housing market you could do equally well just haggling.

Spreading your wings with travel

Possibly the most famous and sought after shareholders' perk ever offered in the UK was by **Eurotunnel**, which awarded its original shareholders three free trips through the Channel tunnel each year.

This attractive gesture sent Eurotunnel shares shooting to a peak of £13 each before wiser counsels prevailed. Those who took profits at the top and reinvested their money elsewhere arguably did much better than those who stayed in for the free rides as the shares collapsed.

With Eurotunnel losing money year after year up to 2006 and calling on shareholders for further investments to keep the company going, the free rides were the only return on the shares. If you did not wish to visit France or Belgium on a regular basis, there was simply no point in buying them.

Much has admittedly changed at Eurotunnel over the years and the financial mess has been sorted out. Holders of at least 1,000 shares for at least three months now get a 30% reduction in the standard fare on up to six one-way or three return journeys a year.

Prices vary enormously depending on when you go and how long you stay across the Channel. You could get a return for as little as £44 or a single ticket for as much as £199 so it is impossible to calculate with any degree of precision the benefit of forking out nearly £6,000 on shares.

Another complication is that Groupe Eurotunnel is now a French rather than an Anglo-French company and its main share listing is in Paris. The shares are traded on the London Stock Exchange but are priced in euros so their value in sterling is affected by changes in the pound/euro exchange rate.

Holidaybreak: A 10% discount on a wide variety of holidays, hotels in the UK and on the Continent looks quite attractive in return for buying 200 shares.

Thomas Cook: A 10% discount on the high street price of holidays and commission-free currency transactions are also attractive provided you like package holidays. This is a better prospect than **TUI**, where you need a minimum of 500 shares and package holiday discounts are capped at £80.

Renishaw: Book a holiday, charter flight or car rental through its Wotton Travel subsidiary and you get a discount, but the amount varies according to what you book so the extent of the perk is somewhat variable.

Much ado about little

Some perks are pretty minimal and even bizarre. Here are some examples:

National Grid: You can ask to go into a ballot to visit company sites and meet directors. It is a chance to get to know the company better but since you have already invested it's a bit late to be doing your homework. Enjoy the pylons.

Associated British Foods: You need only one share but you have to attend the AGM for a free gift, usually a food parcel.

Unilever: Another company that requires attendance at the AGM for a free bag of products plus lunch.

Balfour Beatty: If you agree to receive communications from the company by email it will donate £1 to climate care.

Reckitt Benckiser: Accepting electronic rather than paper communications is worth a £1 donation to the Woodland Trust Tree for All campaign. Or you could save the price of the shares and send £1 to the trust yourself!

EMAP: Some magazines at half price.

Key points

With very few, if any, exceptions, the sensible rules for investors are:

- Do not buy shares just for the perks.

- If you have a choice between qualifying for perks or cutting your dealing costs, opt to cut costs.

- If you decide, on investment grounds, to buy shares that bring perks, make sure you apply for your entitlement.

- If perks are handed out at meetings, check on the company website before you buy the shares as to where and when the AGM is normally held. You need to be sure you can get there.

- Check that the perks are still offered – they can be changed or scrapped.

For full updated lists of shareholder perks visit these websites:

- Barclays Stockbrokers:
  www.stockbrokers.barclays.co.uk/content/ads/documents/Share holder_Brochure.pdf

- Hargreaves Lansdown:
  www.h-l.co.uk/free-guides/shareholder-perks

Chapter 20

International Investing

International companies have a particular appeal to dividend seekers. You can spread risk and choose companies with operations in the fastest growing economies.

You can do this by:

1. investing in UK companies with overseas operations

2. buying shares in companies with a listing on the UK stock market

3. picking companies with listings on overseas stock exchanges.

1. UK companies

The easiest route is through UK companies. You are still in familiar territory, as buying shares in a multinational based here is no different from buying a purely domestic play. Such companies normally report sales and profits in sterling so you do not have to make your own exchange rate calculations.

It does not, one must admit, always work out well, as UK building companies such as Ashtead, Wolseley and Taylor Woodrow discovered when the US housing market that they were so heavily tied in to collapsed.

There have been other instances of transatlantic disasters in both directions. Marks & Spencer had an ill-fated foray into the US by buying American chain Brooks Bros. Supermarket group Sainsbury spent a small fortune on sorting out the Shaw chain it acquired in New England before selling out the moment that Shaw came good.

However, for every shortfall there are several success stories, such as Tesco which has spread gradually into several European countries.

If you invest in a large UK company you are almost certain to be buying into a truly international operation. Nearly 70% of the profits of FTSE 100 companies is earned abroad.

2. Foreign companies listed here

Equally simple is to buy into foreign companies with London listings, as these shares are traded in exactly the same way as UK ones. Dividends will be paid in sterling, again in exactly the same way as for UK companies.

There are, however, added dangers:

1. Foreign companies will almost certainly be governed by different laws.

2. They will be out of reach of UK authorities if they breach UK listing rules.

3. Many choose to have their shares quoted on AIM, where listing rules are less stringent.

4. They are often controlled by oligarchs dependent on political favours back home.

5. Sales, profits and dividends may be calculated in a foreign currency, with the associated greater complication and foreign exchange risk.

These risks are, however, associated with the merits and probity of the companies themselves and not specifically with the payment of any dividend declared.

3. Overseas exchanges

You open up a vast array of extra companies if you are prepared to buy shares on overseas stock exchanges. Stick to well-regulated ones such as New York, the largest and most active stock market in the world with more than 8,000 quoted companies.

Alternatives in Europe include Paris, Frankfurt and Milan.

Dividends will be declared in a foreign currency, most likely US dollars, euros or yen, but you will receive your dividends through your broker in sterling.

Always check with your broker that there will be no problem before buying shares on any overseas exchange.

The disadvantages are:

- Your broker may not offer this facility or may charge you extra commission, although you will not be paying stamp duty so you may well find that trading on overseas exchanges is no more expensive than buying on the London Stock Exchange.

- Research and information is less readily available in the UK, as only the *Financial Times* among British newspapers really covers overseas stocks.

- The value of your shares and dividends will be affected by foreign exchange movements.

There is much merit in spreading geographic risk. The whole world rarely suffers a serious setback at the same time and when it does one part is usually pretty quick to bounce back.

Thus Western advanced nations came through the Asian economic crisis of the 1990s relatively unscathed while the Far East, particularly China, emerged rapidly from the recession of 2009.

Case study: IMI

Engineering has been a shrinking sector in the UK but IMI, a member of the FTSE 100 Index, found a lucrative niche. It makes specialised valves for critical applications – operations that simply cannot be allowed to go wrong. Examples are nuclear power plants and medical facilities.

Other uses for IMI valves include controlling exhaust gases from lorries. These markets are not going to disappear.

IMI's strategy, developed steadily over several years rather than in one dislocating lurch, was to focus on achieving leading positions in niche global markets with products engineered to the specific needs of customers, with 30% of them in the US and the second largest market in Germany. Products would be turned out in low-cost manufacturing countries.

IMI paid a rising dividend but it prudently invested money at the same time.

Table 20.1: financial history for IMI

	2006	2007	2008	2009	2010
EPS (p)	38.3	41.9	54.1	45.8	66.3
Dividend (p)	18.7	20.2	20.7	21.2	26.0
Dividend cover	2.05	2.07	2.61	2.16	2.55

Source: London Stock Exchange

When it produced annual results for 2010 it announced that it was appointing 350 new engineers, of whom 250 would be in emerging markets. The company proposed to invest £45 million over the next three years to drive growth.

The success of the strategy was shown in a 44% increase in pre-tax profits to £304.4 million in the 2010 calendar year on sales up 7% to £1.9 billion. The final dividend of 17p was up 29% from 13.2p in the previous year, making the total payout 26p.

Chart 20.1 – Share price chart for IMI

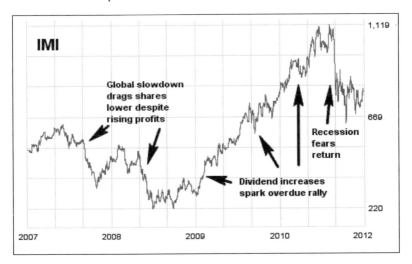

There were excellent buying opportunities for investors along the way, particularly between 2007 and 2009 as the shares were dragged down unfairly by fears of a global recession. They recovered strongly but ran out of steam in 2011 as talk of a double-dip recession in the UK and Europe hit stock markets, thus providing another chance for investors to buy into the success story.

Key points

- Investing in overseas companies broadens your choice of companies and spreads risk.

- You are no longer reliant on the UK economy doing well.

- You can invest in sectors that are under-represented on the London Stock Exchange.

- Investing through well-regulated overseas stock exchanges may be no more expensive than investing in London.

PART D

Building a Dividend Portfolio

Chapter 21

Spotting Buying Opportunities

Because we are buying mainly for the long term we should not get too bogged down in picking the precise moment to buy. The only way to find out if shares have hit the bottom is to look back with hindsight, by which time it is too late.

Nonetheless, we want to spot buying opportunities that will allow us to build a promising portfolio at the lowest cost, or maximise our purchases for a set amount of money.

Buying rumours

There is an old stock market adage that you should buy on rumour and sell on news. This is not a rule to follow too literally, especially if you are a dividend investor, for its message is more about speculative investment and short-term profits. Nonetheless there is an element of sense in the saying that can be turned to advantage by longer-term share buyers.

Mild speculative fever does sometimes build up around a company. There may be unsubstantiated rumours of a takeover, for example, that often come to nothing. The shares run up for several days, only to subside when no bid materialises or the company denies that it has received an approach.

Dividend shareholders should not leap onto the bandwagon in such situations. Leave the short-term gains, and the subsequent tears of those sucked in, to active traders.

Buying on dips

There is one situation, however, where a sharp rise and fall in the share price can be beneficial to dividend investors. This is when speculative buying precedes good results from a company and the speculators take profits as soon as the figures are announced.

Do *not* join in the pre-results frenzy. The speculators could be wrong and you will have ended up paying over the odds for your shares. The opportunity comes when the speculators get it right and the results turn out to be good – yet the results are greeted by a fall in the share price.

It means you have confirmation in the results that all is well plus the opportunity to buy in below recent highs.

Tesco

This has happened on many occasions at Tesco as it progressed from being the UK's second largest retailer behind Sainsbury to easily the largest, producing a string of positive results along the way.

Table 21.1 – Financial history for Tesco

Tesco	2006-7	2007-8	2008-9	2009-10	2010-11
Sales (£m)	42,641	47,298	53,898	56.910	66,931
Pre-tax profits (£m)	2,653	2,803	2,917	3,176	3,535
EPS (p)	22.36	27.37	29.06	31.80	35.90
Dividend (p)	9.64	10.9	11.96	13.05	14.46
Dividend cover	2.32	2.51	2.43	2.44	2.48

Source: London Stock Exchange

Chart 21.1– Share price chart for Tesco

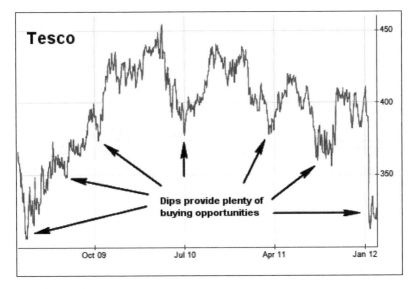

Almost all of the announcements of positive results were greeted with a fall in the share price. That was the time for new investors to buy in.

Case Study: Weir

A member of the FTSE 100 Index, Weir attracted attention in 2010 and 2011 for two good reasons: UK manufacturing was showing a remarkably strong surge as products became more competitive thanks to the weak pound, while companies serving the oil and mining sectors were prospering from high demand for power and raw materials as the world economy recovered from the financial crisis in 2008.

Weir ticked both boxes. The engineering company made pumps and valves for oil, gas, mining and power industries and its technology was particularly important in boosting production from shale oil fields which were being exploited to take advantage of the soaring oil price.

Exceptionally good results were reported for 2010. Revenue was up 18% to £1.64 billion, thanks to a remarkable 50% boost in oil and gas receipts. Even better was the 62% rise in pre-tax profits from £170 million to £277 million. That meant Weir could comfortably pay a final dividend of 21p to take the total payout up 29% to 27p.

Table 21.2 – Financial history for Weir

Weir	2006	2007	2008	2009	2010
Sales (£m)	870.4	1,008.8	1,353.6	1,90.2	1635.0
Profits (£m)	90.5	109.0	159.5	170.4	276.2
EPS (p)	27.8	39.7	59.3	64.1	100.4
Dividend (p)	14.5	16.5	18.5	21.0	27.0
Dividend cover	1.92	2.41	3.21	3.05	3.72

Source: London Stock Exchange

The future looked equally promising, with the order books at record levels. In the oil and gas division the order book was almost double the level it had stood at a year earlier at the start of such a profitable year. The mineral division, although less buoyant, still had orders 26% higher.

Even the power and industrial operations, where clients had been more subdued, saw orders rise 6%.

So Weir started 2011 with enough orders already secured to beat 2010's excellent revenue figures.

As Chief Executive Keith Cochran said in announcing the results, Weir entered 2011 in excellent health with a record order book, a clear strategy and plans for future growth.

Five acquisitions over the previous 12 months had broadened the portfolio of products without straining financial and managerial resources, increasing exposure to high-growth emerging markets.

Chart 21.2 – Share price chart for Weir

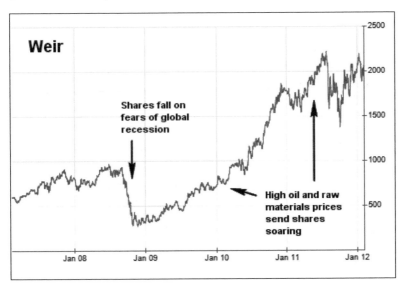

Yet despite all this, Weir shares fell 84p to 1695p on the day the results were released. Based on the 2010 dividend, the yield was 1.6%. While that was not an outstanding yield, it was better than many quoted companies and certainly higher than you could get in an ordinary bank savings account at the time.

More importantly, Weir looked certain to raise the dividend again in the current year, perhaps substantially. Therefore the fall in the share price following the results announcement could have provided a very good buying opportunity for investors interested in the company.

Key points

- Do not be afraid to hold back if you think a surge in the share price has been overdone.

- Do not buy immediately after bad news even if the shares have fallen to a superficially attractive level.

- Look for buying opportunities after good results and trading statements in case short-term buyers take profits.

Chapter 22

Building a Portfolio Using Stock Filters

We learnt in Part C about the *types* of companies we are looking for, but finding specific examples that fit our criteria can be quite daunting.

Where do we begin?

With more than 2,000 companies quoted on the London Stock Exchange, we need some method of quickly filtering out companies that are of no interest to us so that we can sift through a manageable number of suitable candidates.

We can do this the laborious, old-fashioned way by trawling though the share price tables shown in newspapers. This will certainly give us some ideas, and is not to be scoffed at, but you will be able to screen out companies only on the basis of yield and P/E, which are the two columns usually printed in any newspaper that covers the stock market seriously.

But factors we would most want to take into account are:

1. market cap

2. stock market index

3. yield

4. dividend cover

5. dividend growth

6. P/E

7. gearing

8. interest cover.

Online stock screens

Various online financial sites offer a screening facility. These can vary enormously in degree of sophistication and, as always, investors do best by finding one that suits their needs and which they are comfortable with using. Some websites put stock screens within their paid-for services and online brokers usually expect you to register with them.

Stock filter at The Share Centre

A simple example is the Share Center's stock filter. It is free and can be found at **wwwshare.com/cgi-bin/oicgi.exe/inet_tsc_dl_filter2**; or log onto the Share Centre (**www.share.com**) and select 'Research the Markets' > 'Find an investment' > 'Find shares – SharePicker' > 5 Performance. We are directed to this site from the finance section of *The Daily Telegraph* website **www.telegraph.co.uk**.

The page looks like this:

Not important to you	1	2	3	4	5	Important to you
Dividend Yield	1	2	3	4	●5	
P/E Ratio	1	2	3	4	●5	
PEG Ratio	●1	2	3	4	5	
EPS	●1	2	3	4	5	
EPS Growth	1	2	3	4	●5	
Margin	●1	2	3	4	5	

reset   search

If we make some selections (as I have done above), then we get a page like this:

Overview

Find results

change criteria

Companies matching criteria: 5

Your search criteria
Dividend Yield: 5   P/E ratio: 5   PEG ratio: 1   EPS: 1   EPS Growth: 5   Margin: 1

Refine my search and change criteria >>

Click on column title to sort up or down

▼ Name	Sector	Div Yield	P/E	PEG	EPS Adj.	EPS Grth.	Operating Margin	Price
Greenwich Loan Income Fund Ltd.	Equity Inves...	8.65%	3.7	0.0	12.66p	222.96	116.39%	46.25p
HaiKe Chemical Group Ltd. (DI)	Oil & Gas Pr...	6.22%	4.2	0.0	16.40¢	3,180.00	1.99%	43.50p
Invista Real Estate Investment Management Holdings	Financial Se...	8.59%	1.8	0.0	4.47p	91.03	54.86%	8.15p
Lighthouse Group	Financial Se...	6.00%	5.3	0.0	1.14p	850.00	0.29%	6.00p
Ventus 2 VCT	Equity Inves...	6.08%	12.5	0.0	3.29p	430.65	73.11%	41.12p

Selecting on this basis can be helpful but it is rather a blunt instrument.

Stock filter at Interactive Investor

An alternative, and arguably the best available free without having to register with the site, is Interactive Investor site at:
www.iii.co.uk/markets/?type=stockfilter

As we can see, this page gives a range of criteria:

Stock Filter

Apply different criteria to over 3,700 companies to limit your choice of potential investments to a manageable number (which you can then research further).

3885 stocks
currently found

Basic settings

| Sector | Any |
| Index | Any |

Advanced Settings

⊞ Fundamentals (2200 companies)

⊞ Ratios (2200 companies)

⊞ Share data and Performance

⊞ RNS News

Display results (3885 companies)   Reset filter

We can leave the search as wide open as we wish. As the page above stands, we are not restricting our search to any particular sector or index.

However, if, say, we choose banks from the list of sectors and FTSE 100 from the list of indices, then select fundamentals as our basis of selection, we get this:

Stock Filter

Apply different criteria to over 3,700 companies to limit your choice of potential investments to a manageable number (which you can then research further).

Filter currently matches 2 companies

Basic settings

| Sector | Banks |
| Index | FTSE 100 |

Advanced Settings

⊟ Fundamentals (2200 companies)

Criteria	Preset Values	More Than	Less Than	View in Results
Turnover (£m)	Select	1000		☑
Pretax Profit (£m)	Select	1000		☑
Operating Profit (£m)	Select	1000		☑
Market Cap (£m)	Select	1000		☑

Here we have selected minimum values as the basis of our criteria but we could set maximum values in the Less Than column if we wished. We can even set a minimum and a maximum to search between. We note that, on the criteria we have set, two companies fit. By clicking on the Display Results button we find out which two:

Code	Name	Turnover (£m)	Pretax Profit (£m)	Operating Profit (£m)	Market Cap (£m)	Action
HSBA	HSBC Holdings	34,752.75	12,204.62	10,590.97	101,789.69	Buy/Sell
STAN	Standard Chartered	10,297.35	3,924.81	4,512.70	38,334.72	Buy/Sell

Alternatively, the page below shows an example of choosing stocks according to ratios, where we have selected the Household Goods sector and FTSE 250 stocks. We have set criteria for three ratios but left EPS open.

Basic settings				
Sector	Household Goods			
Index	FTSE 250			

Advanced Settings

⊞ Fundamentals (2200 companies)

⊟ Ratios (2200 companies)

Criteria	Preset Values	More Than	Less Than	View in Results
EPS	Select			☐
PE Ratio	Select	5	10	☑
Dividend Yield	Select	5	6	☑
Dividend Cover	Select	2	3	☑
Price To Sales	Select			☐

We can filter according to fundamentals, ratios and share data at the same time but remember that the more criteria you use, that is the more you narrow your selection, the fewer companies are likely to be produced. This is good if we are looking for just one or two companies to top up a portfolio but too restrictive when we are starting out, when we should be aiming for around 20-30 candidates to produce a balanced portfolio of about a dozen stocks.

Leave the sector set at 'any' in the first instance. This filter is useful when we are seeking to balance our portfolio with a company from a sector that is not represented in our existing portfolio.

Commonsense tells you to try setting the criteria and seeing how many stocks come up. You can then widen or narrow the search accordingly. As a dividend investor you will probably want to set minimum standards for yield and dividend cover while leaving other criteria fairly slack.

A sample portfolio

Using the Interactive Investor filter, we could build a very solid and promising portfolio by selecting.

- *Sector Box*: **Any**

- *Index box*: **FTSE 100.**

Click on Ratios and:

- *PE Ratio*: Type **10** in the Less Than box

- *Dividend Yield*: Type **4** in the More Than box

- *Dividend Cover*: Type **2** in the More Than box.

Leave all other boxes blank and click on Display Results. The outcome of performing this exercise on 1 February 2012 was:

Code	Name	PE Ratio	Dividend Yield	Dividend Cover
AZN	AstraZeneca	8.55	5.33	2.20
BLND	British Land	5.12	5.04	3.87
CNA	Centrica	7.54	5.05	2.63
LAND	Land Securities Grp	4.19	4.15	5.76
LGEN	Legal & General Grp	8.21	4.11	2.96
MKS	Marks & Spencer	8.43	5.20	2.28
RSL	Resolution Ltd	3.34	6.66	4.50
SBRY	Sainsbury (J)	8.37	5.24	2.28
SSE	SSE	7.68	6.02	2.16
TSCO	Tesco	9.88	4.42	2.29
UU.	United Utilities	8.94	5	2.24

This gives us a manageable list of 11 stocks fairly well spread across a range of sectors. We note that we have two property companies, British Land and Land Securities, and have the option of dropping one of them in order to avoid overweighting that particular sector in the portfolio. Likewise we have two supermarkets, Sainsbury and Tesco, and can use our judgement if we wish to eliminate one or the other. That still leaves nine shares in a rather pleasing portfolio.

Note that we should not use stock filters to entirely replace our own judgement and commonsense. We should look through the list, decide if we are happy with all of the selections, and ditch any that we feel uncomfortable with.

One disadvantage of this site is that it has a limited range of indices to choose from. If you want the FTSE 350 you have to go through this exercise for the FTSE 100 and the FTSE 250 separately.

Other stock-filtering services

Other sites well worth looking at are:

- **ADVFN (www.advfn.com)**

  You have to register, which is free for basic research. Click on 'Charts & Research' and select 'UK Screener' from the dropdown menu.

- **Digital Look (www.digitallook.com)**

  Offers basic research free but charges a monthly fee for more sophisticated research. You will need to register but you do not have to commit yourself to a subscription. Click on 'Research', then 'Screening Tools', then 'Screener'.

- **Motley Fool (www.foolsharedealing.co.uk)**

  Requires you to register on its share dealing site but you can access its stock screening service, provided by Digital Look, without actually dealing. Click on 'Research Centre', then 'Equities Centre', then 'Stock Screener'.

The Motley Fool page gives access to better research more easily than logging on to Digital Look itself, as the comprehensive page on Motley Fool shown below suggests:

This page gives us more flexibility as it offers a wider range of indices and also allows us to set a minimum stock market capitalisation rather than be restricted to a specific index.

We could have logged into this site on the same day as we visited Interactive Investor (discussed earlier in this chapter) and used different criteria, as follows:

Key Fields

Field	min	max	unit
Market Cap	500		mil
Revenue			mil
Operating Profit/Loss			mil
P/E		9	
PEG			
Price to Sales Ratio			
Dividend Yield	5		%
Dividend Growth (Average)	2		% 1 Year
EPS Growth (Average)	2		% 1 Year
Operating Margin			%
Return on Capital Employed (ROCE)			%

This exercise would have given us 14 stocks:

↑ Name	Market Cap (m)	Avg Div. Grth. 1yr	Div Yield	Avg EPS Grth. 1yr	P/E	Price	30 Day Chg	P/E
AstraZeneca	£40,496.07	10.87%	5.30%	6.17%	7.2	3,048.50p	2.47%	7.2
Aviva	£10,151.89	6.25%	7.30%	22.17%	6.3	355.50p	18.18%	6.3
Beazley	£726.46	3.47%	8.35%	45.67%	5.2	142.10p	5.81%	5.2
Brown (N.) Group	£651.89	15.01%	5.40%	9.08%	8.5	234.20p	0.56%	8.5
Carillion	£1,329.06	6.16%	5.02%	5.63%	7.8	311.00p	3.39%	7.8
Dairy Farm International Holdings Ltd. (Singapore)	$1,010.17	12.50%	24.00%	12.88%	2.5	$0.75	0.00%	2.5
Drax Group	£1,939.25	133.58%	6.02%	10.34%	8.3	532.50p	-2.29%	8.3
FirstGroup	£1,493.58	7.12%	7.14%	5.91%	7.5	312.00p	-7.69%	7.5
Halfords Group	£630.36	10.00%	6.90%	8.82%	7.4	325.20p	12.53%	7.4
ICAP	£2,197.65	13.68%	5.94%	12.71%	8.4	358.10p	3.23%	8.4
Intermediate Capital Group	£1,100.52	5.88%	6.55%	30.40%	8.4	286.00p	25.00%	8.4
Ladbrokes	£1,286.41	155.04%	5.36%	113.82%	3.1	146.10p	12.38%	3.1
Telefonica SA	€59,696.40	30.00%	9.82%	31.58%	5.9	€13.44	1.45%	5.9
TUI Travel	£2,138.75	2.73%	5.91%	24.21%	8.1	195.10p	17.67%	8.1

Again we get a range of sectors.

Two companies are quoted in foreign currencies and we would remove them from the list if we wanted to stick with purely UK companies. The travel industry had recently been under considerable pressure with a profit warning from Thomas Cook and the sinking of a Carnival Group cruise ship in the Mediterranean so we would exercise our judgement as to whether to exclude TUI. Likewise we might be uncomfortable with including two retail groups, N Brown and Halfords, given the difficulties being felt across the sector with prices rising and disposable incomes being squeezed.

Key points

- Stock filters allow you to find a range of stocks to fit your investment criteria.

- You can widen or narrow the criteria to produce a larger or smaller range of candidates.

- When starting out, do not restrict your choice to a particular sector.

- If you are adding to an existing portfolio, consider narrowing the search to a specific sector that is not represented in your holdings.

Chapter 23
Dogs Might Fly

We can use stock filters to follow a strategy known as the *Dogs of the Dow*. This was the nickname given to an investment idea devised by Michael O'Higgins who attempted to identify undervalued, high-yielding stocks that were relatively risk free. It may sound too good to be true but there is much to commend his notion.

O'Higgins identified the ten stocks in the Dow Jones Industrial Average (DJIA) with the highest prospective yields and suggested investing equal amounts of money in the five with the lowest share prices. He reckoned that the market tends to overdo the gloom in such situations and there are therefore good prospects of recovery in the share price.

O'Higgins set an arbitrary time limit of one year, during which time the shares should not be sold. At the end of a year the exercise would be repeated, with shares that no longer qualified being sold and new 'dogs' being bought.

In favour of this system:

- The system can be adapted to any major index on any reputable stock exchange.

- You can invest in as few or as many companies as you wish – it does not have to be five.

- You can choose the criteria for whittling down the number of companies, for example, by making the five those with the highest yields or the ones with the lowest P/E ratios.

- You can reject companies where you suspect that analysts will downgrade their forecast, thus reducing the prospective yield.

Against:

- No system gives winners every time.

Alert readers may have spotted another flaw in this system as far as dividend investors are concerned: despite the main criterion being a high prospective yield, this system was devised primarily to produce capital gains.

Nonetheless, we can adapt it to our needs.

Adapting the O'Higgins system

The general principle of seeking high yielding stocks among the largest companies is a good place for any dividend investor to start because larger companies are more likely than smaller ones to:

1. pay and maintain dividends

2. have the resources to cope better in difficult economic conditions

3. be able to attract a better calibre of executive to turn the company round if it is struggling.

Second, we need not think in terms of using a rigid formula to choose which high-yielding large companies to invest in. We can pick the best prospects using fundamental data.

Third, we do not have to hold the shares for a year and then feel forced to part with those that have recovered strongly. We can use our investment acumen to decide to retain the shares if we wish.

Finally, and most importantly, we hope to enjoy a high yield on our shares from the word go.

Finding which shares have the highest yields

Strictly speaking, the comparable UK index to the Dow Jones Industrial Average is the FT30. Like the DJIA, the FT30 comprises the 30 largest companies listed on the relevant stock exchange.

However, it is reasonable to substitute the FTSE 100 Index, which has largely superseded the FT 30 and which contains a broader range of market sectors while retaining the fundamental approach of selecting on very large companies.

The best way of finding high yielding shares in the FTSE 100 is to log on to one of the online stock filters, and select the FTSE 100 Index as the universe to search on. Depending on the facility on the stock screener you are using you can rank by highest yield or set a minimum yield, adjusting the figure to increase or reduce the number of candidates as appropriate.

You can, if you wish, widen this concept to the FTSE 350 Index, thus adding in the midcaps, but you should exercise great caution if you do. You may identify possible investment opportunities but you are getting away from the O'Higgins' concept of choosing from only large companies.

It is extremely risky to widen further to the All Share Index as you will be including smaller companies that are more likely to scrap their dividends in tough times.

If you are not computer-savvy or if the website you use does not have this facility or charges a fee for it, then you can still get the information you need from newspapers. It is just that doing the job manually is more time consuming.

All newspapers carrying stock market tables identify FTSE 100 companies, either by putting them in bold or by a symbol. You need to work your way through finding those with the highest figures in the yield column. The big advantage of this method is that it makes you think. You can easily disregard stocks with a potentially high yield that you feel are about to come a cropper and list the ones you are more comfortable with.

Note that you cannot use *The Daily Telegraph* for this exercise; it uses historic yields in its tables.

Key points

- The O'Higgins method was intended to identify potential capital gains but it adapts well to dividend investing.

- The system identifies undervalued large companies.

- Remember that no system produces winners all the time.

Chapter 24
Income Funds

There is an argument for investing in a fund that specialises in producing dividends. On the whole, I encourage investors to make their own judgements and investment decisions. Indeed, this book is intended to help investors to do just that.

However, we can consider the pros and cons of investing through an investment trust, a unit trust or an open-ended investment company, all of which pool the resources of thousands of small investors and use a professional to create wealth.

Two types of fund

Closed funds

Investment trusts are closed funds. A fixed number of shares are issued when the fund is set up, as with any company quoted on the stock market. New shares can by issued only with the consent of existing shareholders.

These trusts operate just like any quoted company. The only real difference is that they do not operate businesses themselves, they invest in other companies. As an investor, you buy shares from existing shareholders and sell to new investors. Supply and demand in the market decides the price of the shares.

Shares in investment trusts tend to trade at a discount to the trusts assets. This means that the stock market capitalisation of the trust is less than the aggregate value of the cash, shares, bonds and any other assets it owns.

Investment trusts tend to have finite lives and the discount reflects the cost of selling the assets and distributing cash raised to the shareholders. It also provides a safety net in case the value of the assets fall. However, it does mean that new investors are buying in at a bargain price.

Open funds

Unit trusts and OEICs are open ended, in that there is no fixed number of units. If an investor wants to put money into the fund, new units are created. When an investor sells, the trust buys in the units and cancels them.

Since there is no stock market mechanism for setting the price, the fund manager decides each day at what price units can be bought and sold. The aim is to set a price that will balance supply and demand.

The size of the fund thus expands and contracts with demand. If the units are under-priced and investors pile in, the fund will find itself with surplus cash. If the price is set too high and sellers cash in, then it may be necessary to sell assets in order to meet the payments.

Advantages and disadvantages of funds

In favour:

- The professional should do better than you.

- You spread your risks in one fell swoop.

- You can still run your own (individual company) satellite portfolios in addition to the fund.

- Some funds give you access to foreign stocks.

Against:

- The professional has to earn his or her fees on top of giving you a decent return.

- No-one else knows your investment criteria as well as you do.

- You miss out on all the fun of making your own decisions.

Some funds have served investors over many years, paying increased dividends. While such sterling performance is encouraging we should remember the adage that past performance is not necessarily a guide to what will happen in the future. Table 24.1 gives a sample of investment trusts that have paid rising dividends for a number of years, their total return over the past five years and their yield at 30 September, 2011.

Table 24.1 – Sample of investment trusts with history of rising dividends

	Rising divs	Total return	Yield
City of London	45 years	18%	4.9%
Alliance	44 years	6%	2.6%
Albany	42 years	- 3%	4.3%

Source: *The Daily Telegraph* Money section, 30 September 2011

Quite a long list of investment trusts have increased their dividends over many years. They include Caledonia for 44 years, F&C Smaller Companies for 41 years, JP Morgan Claverhouse for 38 years, Witan for 36 years and Scottish Mortgage for 29 years.

This has been great news for those wanting a regular, rising income. However, those seeking to build wealth may be more interested in total returns, where our table shows the performance to be more patchy.

Investment trusts – and the same argument applies to unit trusts and OEICs – that concentrate on producing income may invest heavily in defensive stocks and miss opportunities to catch cyclical stocks on the rise.

By paying out regular and increasing dividends they also reduce their potential for reinvesting cash to give greater long-term total returns.

The price of units in open-ended funds such as unit trusts or shares in closed funds such as investment trusts can go up or down in line with the stock market. There is no guarantee that you will get back your original investment in full when the time comes to sell.

Where to get information

If you want to start your investment career by buying into an investment company then you should visit the website of the Association of Investment Companies (**www.theaic.co.uk**) which contains fact sheets on all member companies. These will give you a flavour of each fund's investment criteria and past performance.

Click on 'Search for an Investment Company' and select 'Step-by-Step Approach', then 'Conventional Companies'. Pick a region and then select Income to reach a page such as this:

http://www.theaic.co.uk/Search-for-an-investment-company/Step-by-step-search/

Taking one such company, Henderson High Income, at random, gives a flavour of the type of investment portfolio that is likely to be held. The figures are given in the fund's half-year report to June 2011:

Table 24.2 – Sector breakdown for Henderson High Income

Sector	Weighting(%)
Financials	26.7
Utilities	14.3
Industrials	10.8
Consumer Goods	10.4
Telecommunications	8.4
Oil & Gas	6.0
Consumer Services	4.1
Healthcare	3.2
Fixed Interest Investments	16.1

Table 24.3: Top ten holdings for Henderson High Income

Company	Shares held (m)	Yield(%)
British American Tobacco	8,220	4.2
Vodafone	6,336	5.4
BP	5,733	1.8
GlaxoSmithKline	4,762	5.0
National Grid	4,685	5.9
HSBC	4,380	3.7
Catlin	4,202	6.6
Aviva	4,096	5.8
Jardine Lloyd Thompson	4,086	3.3
Northumbrian Water	3,740	3.4

Income or growth?

You will usually gather from a fund's name whether it aims specifically to produce dividend income or whether it is seeking long-term growth. Either way the fund will be seeking to invest in companies that pay regular and rising dividends. The big difference is that an income fund hands over some or all of the dividends it receives to its own shareholders by paying its own dividend. A growth fund reinvests the dividends it receives.

Which type of fund you prefer will depend on what stage you are at. If you are looking for income then you will obviously want an income fund; if your hope is that all income will be rolled up in further investments then you want a growth fund.

Table 24.4: Income or growth

Examples of income funds	Examples of growth funds
Aberdeen Asian Income	Biotech Growth Trust
Edinburgh New Income	Finsbury Growth
Global Special Opportunities Income	Global Special Opportunities Growth
Hand High Income	JPM Euro Growth
Invesco Property Income	
JPM Euro Inc	
M&G High Income	
Shires Income	

Funds offer variety

We can see that within this small sample of investment trusts we have a wide choice. We can easily find suitable trusts that invest within the UK, Europe, Asia or globally; we can also find some trusts that specialise in particular sectors such as property.

If you have a limited amount to invest, by all means start with an investment trust, unit trust or an OEIC. It should give you a stable basis in case your own judgements fall short.

It can also be suitable for those with substantial sums to invest. If you have one or two solid investments in funds you can, if you wish, take some riskier punts in your own share portfolio.

Key points

- You can use managed funds as a relatively safe central focus and build your own satellite portfolios around it.

- Funds give you a wide spread of investments to hedge your risk.

- Some funds offer easy access to overseas markets where you may be less confident of handling your own investments.

Chapter 25
When to Sell

We have, quite rightly, concentrated on buying opportunities because dividend investors should be looking to the long term. It is important to remember that you are investing principally, or entirely, for dividends and you should not allow yourself to be distracted by swings in share prices.

You will see many swings in both directions over a lifetime of investing. Like water, the stock market gradually finds its own level.

Do not make the mistake, as so many investors do, of being panicked into selling shares after heavy falls as you are likely to be getting out at the bottom of the market and will be forced to buy back in at higher levels.

However, that is not an excuse for burying your head in the sand. Unless you are a very shrewd or a very lucky investor there will be times when you have to face reality and consider selling one of your holdings and reinvesting in a better prospect.

Reasons for deciding to sell include:

- The company's growth period seems to be coming to a close.

- The shares have soared and you believe you can get a better yield by taking profits and investing elsewhere.

- You fear that management is overstretching the resources.

These points are matters of judgement. It is a constant theme of this book that you should keep abreast of the facts, do your research and back your own judgement.

If we feel that there is a serious risk of the dividend being reduced or suspended then it is best to look elsewhere before the rot sets in. We may boost our income considerably if we find a better investment.

Otherwise, when the first warning signs occur it is probably best to err on the side of holding on. Issues can be addressed by management and at this stage it is unlikely that the dividend will be reduced or scrapped. Where a company runs out of steam it is rare indeed for the shares to collapse all at once. There are usually warning signs, with the share price slipping gradually and upward blips along the way to present selling opportunities.

Monitor the company day by day. If the shares persist in slipping when the market generally is holding up, it is an indicator that other investors have the same worries that you have. You should not sit back bemoaning the fact that you missed your chance to get out at the top. Better to sell at a slightly lower price than to wait for the shares to fall further.

Above all, do not cling on to a company out of misplaced loyalty. The company is there to serve you, the shareholder.

Rather more serious reasons for switching investments is if:

- the latest trading statement is gloomy
- the company has issued a profit warning.

When this happens, it is more likely that the dividend will be reduced. Bad news tends to come in batches and a company that issues one warning will almost certainly issue a second and probably a third. The longer that the bad news persists, the more likely it is that the directors will be unable to maintain the dividend.

Gloomy trading statements

Gloomy trading statements are a sort of halfway house between a nagging worry and a full-blown profit warning. We should read all the quarterly trading statements that companies issue and look for telltale signs that tougher times lie ahead.

We're looking first and foremost for whether the statement says that trading is at least in line with market expectations.

Note the phrase 'market expectations'. This suggests that forecasts and the share price are roughly in the right place. This is not the same as saying that trading is in line with 'management expectations', which carries a veiled hint that analysts could be wide of the mark.

Statements to be wary of include:

- 'Trading is falling short of previous guidance.'

- 'Conditions in the markets where the company sells its products have become more difficult.'

- 'Customers are delaying purchases.'

- 'Margins are under pressure.'

- 'Raw material costs are rising strongly.'

- 'The weather has affected sales.'

Remember that company directors, being human, are likely to accentuate the positive so indications of a deterioration of trading may be quite muted in the early stages.

Where trading turns down more gradually, it is unlikely that the share price will fall heavily at first, and there will be occasional upward blips in the share price chart, so there will be opportunities to sell even if you failed to get out at the top.

That is not, however, an excuse for dithering. Once you start to worry about a company it is probably time to take your profits and find another berth. At the very least keep your investment under intensive care.

Profit warnings

In the case of an outright profit warning, the shares will fall, perhaps quite heavily, before we have a chance to cut our losses.

We must turn our skills to extracting the best price we can for our holdings. Our options are:

1. Stick it out in the hope and expectation that the company will come good again.

2. Sell immediately and switch as quickly as possible into a company that does pay a dividend.

3. Hang on with the intention of seizing a better price for our shares in the not too distant future.

Our decision will be affected first and foremost by how hopeful we are that the dividend will be maintained.

1. Sticking it out

This is the most tempting of the options but probably the one that works worst. At the very least it masks our inability to admit our misjudgement in staying with the company for too long.

Hard as it is to admit that we made a mistake, it is far more expensive to cling on when all the evidence suggests that an investment has not worked out.

The dividend investor is not, admittedly, a short-term gambler seeking to get in and out of shares and it can be right to ride out a temporary setback as long as there are good grounds to believe that normal service will be resumed in the next year or so. Obviously, the longer the hiatus is likely to last the greater the need to face reality.

2. Selling immediately

This limits the damage. It is true that we pass up the chance to capitalise on any dead cat bounce in the shares but neither do we risk suffering a further collapse in the shares.

While it is foolish to act in panic, developing a habit of decisive action is a good trait to have.

We should not blind ourselves to impending disaster and it is usually right to sell out, even at a much reduced share price, and switch into a company that does pay a well-covered dividend rather than see a slice of our income disappear altogether.

Do not put your head in the sand. You need to assess the situation by asking yourself these questions:

1. Are the problems short term or long term?

2. Have failing managers been replaced?

3. Is the dividend likely to be scrapped or reduced?

4. If the dividend has been scrapped, are there any indications of when it will be restored?

5. Should we assume that the dividend will be restored at a lower level than before (which is highly likely)?

6. Will a progressive dividend policy be possible when the troubles are over?

The first question is crucial. If there is little or no prospect of sorting things out then we need to bite the bullet and move on. Long-term problems will surely mean a suspension of the dividend and then we will be sitting on dead money that will be earning nothing.

To hold on in the hope that the share price will recover is to be deflected from our purpose of seeking dividends rather than capital gains – and the capital gains may not happen anyway.

3. Holding on for a better selling opportunity

This is a very risky strategy and one that runs contrary to the ethos of dividend investing. In effect, you are hoping for a capital gain (or a reduction of your capital loss) rather than making the dividend your priority.

This is also an excuse for dithering. The chances are that you will take any dead cat bounce as a signal that the worst is over and decide to hang on for a recovery that never comes.

Case study: HMV

Record and bookshop owner HMV had a torrid time in the early years after the millennium with retailing generally under pressure, music piracy running out of control and book sales being poached by supermarkets. Various initiatives to stem the tide met with little success.

However, finances were gradually pulled round by a new management team and dividend investors could be forgiven for taking a punt on HMV maintaining its recovery. Earnings in the year to April 2006 barely covered the dividend but for four years the payout was maintained and cover improved, albeit not reaching comfortable levels.

Table 25.1 – Financial history for HMV

HMV	2006–7	2007–8	2008–9	2009–10	2010–11
EPS (p)	8.2	10.1	11.1	11.7	3.8
Dividend (p)	7.4	7.4	7.4	7.4	0.9
Dividend cover	1.10	1.36	1.5	1.58	4.22

Source: London Stock Exchange

Chart 25.1 – Share price chart for HMV

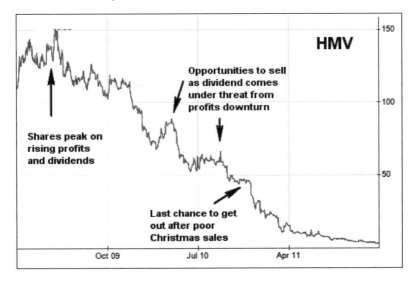

However, the picture started to deteriorate towards the end of the 2009-10 financial year and the shares slid as profit warnings proliferated. HMV attempted to get out of the hole through acquisitions: £7 million cash for a digital media company then £46 million on Mama, the owner of concert venues including the Hammersmith Apollo.

This time the shares fell faster than in 2005-7, losing more than 90% of their value during the two years that Robert Swannell was chairman. When he stepped down at the beginning of March 2011 he declared that his role had become more time consuming. Critics suggested that the company clearly had needed more of his time in the first place.

Certainly it was a warning to investors when he accepted the chairmanship of Marks & Spencer half-way through his term at HMV. Two such demanding jobs surely were bound to leave him overstretched.

When you really must face reality

Whatever reasons any dividend investors might have dredged up to persuade themselves to stay in, they vanished right at the start of 2011 when HMV issued a profit warning after poor Christmas sales.

HMV was not alone among retailers in being affected by the heavy snowfalls that preceded and lasted throughout that festive season, nor is it alone in depending very heavily on Christmas present buying for much of its annual profits. Lost Christmas sales cannot be recovered.

The gloomy news was accompanied by a claim that suppliers were giving the company their full support.

This is the City equivalent of a football club facing relegation saying that the manager has the club's full backing. No one should believe it. Would you, as a supplier to a struggling company, continue to offer credit terms or would you demand payment up front?

We all know the answer.

HMV's debts rose as suppliers demanded earlier payments, putting a further strain on working capital. Credit insurers, who reimburse suppliers if clients go bankrupt, cut back on the amount of insurance they were prepared to provide. It thus became even more urgent for suppliers to reduce their exposure to HMV.

Swannell admitted as he stepped down in March 2011 that debt would reach £130 million, nearly £60 million more than analysts had been expecting, by the time banking covenants were due to be tested the following month.

He further admitted that the retailer was likely to breach those covenants. In these circumstances banks usually charge up-front fees to renew the debts and impose higher interest rates. It is virtually impossible to continue to use precious cash resources to retain the dividend in such circumstances.

HMV faced two options, both highly unpalatable for dividend investors:

1. Make a rights issue, which would force shareholders to throw good money after bad or see their holdings diluted.

2. Sell Waterstones, the better performing half of the business, which would reduce earnings and cash flow and thus jeopardise the dividend.

Business advisers KPMG were called in to help to avert breaching banking covenants and to negotiate with the banks. This meant that HMV was involved in paying advisers just when it most needed to preserve cash. You can be quite sure that business advisers are expensive and they get paid first.

What KPMG did achieve was to persuade the banks to postpone the testing of banking covenants, due at the end of April, for two months. No-one need be fooled by this manoeuvre. The clear implication was that everyone knew the test would be failed and postponing it changed nothing.

To confirm this gloomy analysis, HMV issued its third profit warning in less than four months, saying that conditions in the High Street remained difficult and that profits for the year to the end of April would be £30 million, less than half that for the previous 12 months.

Eventually, in May 2011, HMV sold Waterstones 'to buy time' to sort out the music stores.

Any dividend investors who remained shareholders throughout the long line of disappointments or bought in at some point in the fanciful belief that things could not get any worse had only themselves to blame. The warning signs had been there for long enough.

Stop losses

The whole concept of running stop losses is a highly contentious one, all the more so when applied to dividend investing.

The basic idea is that when you buy shares you set a price at which you will sell out should the share price fall. So if you bought at 100p and the shares fall to, say, 90p, you automatically sell them. Thus if you made a poor purchase you have limited your losses.

Many quite experienced investors swear by stop losses and you may have a friend who talks knowledgably on the subject and scorns those who fail to take this simple precaution as if they were fools. Just nod sagely and keep your own counsel.

There are many drawbacks to setting a stop loss. Here are the most important:

1. Even among those who use stop losses, opinion varies greatly as to how far below the purchase price you should set it.

2. Stop losses force you to sell at a loss, albeit with the aim of limiting the loss, and you miss out if the shares bounce back.

3. Setting a stop loss suggests that you do not have confidence in your own judgement.

4. Dividend investors are not worried about short-term share price movements. Your main concern is that the company pays dividends and if it does the shares will eventually rise in value again.

5. Avoid doing anything automatically. If shares fall, look at the data and at recent announcements from the company to see if you have overlooked anything. Then take an informed judgement on whether to sell or hold on.

So, while stop losses may be a useful tool for short-term traders, their use for long-term investors is much more in doubt.

Key points

- Monitor closely any company whose shares are seriously underperforming the market.

- Do not be panicked into selling by short-term volatility in the stock market but do be realistic about prospects for any individual companies in your portfolio.

- Your main concern is whether there is a serious risk that the dividend will be reduced or suspended.

Chapter 26
A Dividend Nightmare – BP

No book on investing for dividends can possibly be complete without an analysis of the debacle that was BP, once the largest company by stock market capitalisation in the FTSE 100.

BP was a highly successful company with a progressive dividend policy. However, it provided a warning that no investment is without its risks and that unforeseen forces can derail even the most solid-looking company.

Why private investors were at an advantage

BP provided about one-sixth of the income of UK pension funds before disaster struck in the Gulf of Mexico. This is quite astonishing. To have so many of your eggs in one basket runs entirely contrary to perceived investment wisdom.

In this respect, ordinary investors were for once at an advantage over fund managers, who tend to be restricted to large companies, especially those in the FTSE 100 Index, which are regarded as particularly sound.

Also, funds with millions or even billions to invest will tend to pick larger companies. They cannot invest heavily in small companies without pushing the share price sharply higher as they build their stakes, nor disinvest without pushing the share price sharply lower. Thus, for funds, comparatively small percentage stakes in the largest companies are much more manageable.

Small private investors had no excuse for being so over-committed to one specific company. The rule of thumb that you should spread risk by investing fairly equally in ten to a dozen companies in different sectors really came into its own.

Indeed, after disaster struck so unexpectedly, private investors did not have to be invested in BP at all, unlike fund managers running FTSE 100 tracker funds who have no option but to hold shares in blue chips.

The explosion

The initial cause of BP's troubles was the explosion at the Deepwater Horizon oil rig in April 2010, killing 11 people. Apart from the human cost, the leakage of oil from the ocean floor was an environmental disaster and threatened the livelihoods of fishermen in Louisiana and Florida.

At the height of the storm, BP had 48,000 people working on the clean up – even a year on there were still 2,000 people employed mopping up what was left of the oil spill.

A somewhat tawdry blame game followed. BP naturally felt that Transocean, an American company that owned the Deepwater Horizon oil rig and was acting as contractor, and Haliburton, another contractor at the site, should at least share the responsibility but American politics took over. With President Obama and US regulators under fire for allegedly cosying up to BP and failing to insist on adequate safety measures, it became imperative to shift the blame on to the British company.

Why the dividend had to go

Whatever the rights and wrong of apportioning responsibility, BP was the one in the firing line and matters were not helped by the pronouncements of BP Chief Executive Tony Hayward, who seemed to be making light of the disaster. To be fair, whatever he said was likely to be wrong. Stressing the seriousness of the issue would have risked a devastating effect on the BP share price and encouraged litigants to bump up their claims.

Naturally the BP share price fell heavily and sharply anyway, although there were opportunities for alert investors to get out before the worst of the fall. As so often happens, the full impact of events took time to be fully reflected in the share price.

In particular, BP clung on for some time to the hope that it could retain its dividend. Here is another important point for investors to remember: wishful thinking often gets the better of company chiefs when they come under fire.

Eventually it became clear that it was politically unfeasible for BP to continue paying dividends while American victims of the blowout were demanding compensation. If BP had money to throw at shareholders, then the pressure for compensation would be intense.

Dividend investors had plenty of warning that the dividend would be suspended well before it happened. They were also warned by BP when it finally faced reality that the suspension would be indefinite and that when the dividend was restored it would be at a lower level than previously.

The dangers of buying back in

Some analysts and financial journalists suggested, with suspect logic, that BP had become an attractive investment now that the shares were at a lower level and the company was essentially still strong. These siren voices claimed that all would be back to normal soon.

However, for dividend investors, the shares were far from attractive. The share price had fallen by a third, which was inadequate compensation for enduring a period of no income followed by a period of reduced income. A more reasonable assessment was to argue that the shares needed to have lost half their value, not just one-third, to compensate.

Chart 26.1 – Share price chart for BP

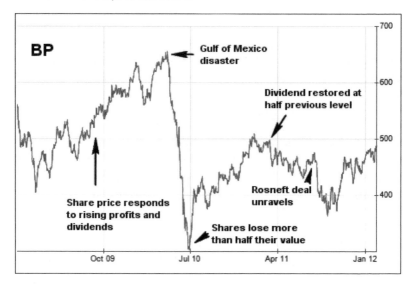

However, the enforced removal of Hayward as chief executive and the emergence of Bob Dudley in his stead brought hope that the whole episode could be brushed aside within a fairly short time scale and that dividends could be quickly restored to earlier levels.

Dudley had one considerable advantage: he was American, a man from Mississippi, one of the worst affected states. He had the potential to defuse the transatlantic row and appease the anti-British faction.

Unfortunately, controversy over the oil spill continued to dog BP long after the clean up had been completed, with allegations that insufficient attention has been paid to safety concerns on the Gulf and elsewhere.

In January 2011 the Mississippi attorney general filed a court case alleging that the compensation fund was intentionally underpaying victims and was delaying payments to force litigants to accept low settlements. US investigators hinted at corporate manslaughter charges.

The long after-effects were quite enough in themselves to make investors cautious of investing in BP, especially as Shell offered quite an attractive alternative.

Why you should fear the worst

It is possible for a new man to walk in and sort out a mess. Few people are likely to stand in his way and the hopes and prayers of the entire company will be behind him. Indeed, even the person who created the mess can sometimes extricate himself and the company from the mire.

However, it is best to work on the assumption that no fairy godmother will wave a magic wand and turn the pumpkin into a crystal coach. The best you can usually hope for is a long slog in which the damage is repaired at considerable cost over many months and the dividend suffers in the meantime.

Something rather worse happened at BP. Instead of meticulously restoring BP's battered reputation, Dudley launched an ambitious deal that was suspect from the start: a £10 billion share swap and Arctic exploration alliance with Russian oil giant Rosneft, which had been awarded drilling rights in the Kara Sea off northern Siberia.

One can see the superficial attraction. Russia has oil and gas aplenty and the Rosneft deal gave BP access to an area the size of the North Sea in one of the world's most promising regions.

There were certain drawbacks:

1. Rosneft was controlled by the Kremlin, making this a dangerous political liaison. The actions of Russia's political elite could be unpredictable.

2. The terms of the deal were generous to Rosneft, which would become the largest shareholder in BP with 5%.

3. BP risked upsetting AAR, its Russian partners in its TNK–BP joint venture.

4. BP had already had a torrid time of it in Russia. Relations with AAR had been difficult and in 2008 Dudley, then TNK-BP's chief executive, had been forced to flee Russia after a bust-up.

5. AAR argued that its agreement with BP stipulated that both firms must use TNK-BP as their primary vehicle for exploration in Russia.

To drive home its point, AAR blocked the payment of dividends by TNK-BP, thus depriving BP of £1.1 billion in revenue. Under a shareholder's agreement, both sides had to approve any dividends.

A London court granted an injunction to freeze the Rosneft deal pending an arbitration tribunal. The ruling coincided with annual results showing that BP made a full-year loss of £3.1 billion, with lower than expected profits in the fourth quarter. However, the quarterly dividend was restored, although at half its previous level.

Attempts to negotiate a deal with AAR failed acrimoniously as an arbitration tribunal in Sweden ruled in favour of AAR.

How one piece of bad news leads to another

As this saga developed, more Russian oligarchs came forward to add fuel to the fire. Yukos, formerly Russia's biggest oil producer, claimed to be the real owner of 80% of Rosneft's assets.

Yukos said that most of its oilfields had been 'stolen' after fraud charges were brought against its head, Mikhail Khodorovsky, in a trial widely condemned in the West.

Then Gazprom, Russia's state-owned energy giant, was able to buy TNK-BP's Kovykta field, the largest undeveloped gas field in the country, at a ludicrously low price after the Kremlin put too many obstacles in the way for TNK-BP to develop the field. This was a stark reminder to BP shareholders that their company was trying to do business with a country where normal rules did not apply.

Eventually, in May 2011, the Rosneft deal fell apart as the deadline for signing passed without a compromise emerging. Very quickly Rosneft signed a deal with Exxon, leaving BP out in the cold.

When you are down, everyone wants to kick you. Other issues to arise as BP struggled were:

- a renewed allegation that it had manipulated the US gas market

- a threat of corporate manslaughter charges in the US over the Gulf explosion

- an acrimonious AGM at which some protestors had to be ejected

- a fall in profits for the first quarter of 2011, despite the soaring oil price, because of lower output

- a £15 million fine following two oil spills in Alaska.

When a company the size of BP gets into difficulties there is a temptation to believe that it is too big to fail. You take this view at your peril. BP remained singularly unattractive to dividend investors for well over a year after the Gulf of Mexico oil spill.

Timeline

2010

- **April 20:** Oil rig explodes in Gulf of Mexico, killing 11 people and sending oil spewing from the floor of the ocean.

- **July 21:** Dividend suspended

- **July 15:** Well is finally capped after several failed attempts.

- **July 27:** BP says Tony Hayward will step down as chief executive on 1 October and is to be replaced by Bob Dudley.

- **Summer:** US authorities launch criminal investigation into Gulf oil spill.

2011

- **January:** Mississippi attorney files court case alleging underhand tactics to persuade litigants to accept lower settlements.

- **Mid-January:** BP strikes deal with Rosneft to explore Kara Sea area in northern Siberia. Yukos, another Russian oil producer, claims that 80% of the Rosneft assets were illegally seized from Yukos and sold at artificially low prices.

- **Late January:** Partners in TNK-BP block payment on dividends from the joint venture, denying BP £1.1 billion due in February. Two days later London court blocks Rosneft deal pending talks and further hearings.

- **1 February:** BP reports its first full-year loss since 1992 and puts its troubled Texas City refinery up for sale. The dividend is restored at half its previous level.

- **Late February:** Florida lawsuit alleging negligence and fraud against compensation fund.

- **1 March:** Gazprom buys TNK-BP's prize Kovykta gas field at a knock-down price.

- **25 March:** Arbitration tribunal in Sweden rules that Rosneft agreement violates previous agreement with TNK-BP partners.

- **Late March:** Fears of corporate manslaughter charges in US.

- **14 April:** Protesters including Americans affected by Gulf of Mexico oil spill are ejected from stormy Annual General Meeting just before first anniversary of the disaster.

- **27 April:** Crude oil hits $125 a barrel, BP shares trade around 460p, down by a third since the accident, as first quarter profits fall.

- **17 May:** Rosneft deal lapses.

Key points

- Even a company as big as BP can run into trouble.

- Management may compound the problems by acting hastily.

- Any upward blips in the share price presented an opportunity to get out.

Chapter 27
Ten Dividend Rules

1. Spread risk

It is the first rule of investment and it applies particularly to dividend investors. We are not here for a quick killing, nor are we thirsting for the excitement of the casino table.

Diversification to diminish risk is particularly important for income-seekers who cannot afford to lose capital or see the stream of income dry up.

2. Look for sustainable long-term growth

Dividend investors are not looking to chop and change or to cash in quick profits so it follows that you want companies and sectors with genuine continuous prospects for profits, cash flow and, hence, dividends.

Better still if you can get in before other investors spot the company's potential, but in that case you need to do your research and satisfy yourself that the company really has been overlooked and is not being ignored for good reason.

3. Seek reliability

Look for defensive stocks rather than cyclicals. Defensive stocks are the ones that plod along making reasonable but unspectacular profits whatever the economic circumstances.

No sector or company is entirely immune from the economic cycle although some are more susceptible than others. Defensive stocks will tend to rise and fall with the cycle but as dividend investors we are not primarily concerned about share price movements.

Companies making solid profits will have scope to at least maintain the dividend in tough economic times while increasing the payout when the going gets easier. Examples include pharmaceuticals, which enjoy an expanding market as the population ages in developed areas of the world and standards of living and medical care improve in emerging markets. If you are not squeamish about 'unethical' investments, you can include tobacco companies.

4. Don't be distracted by short-term trends

If we pick reliable companies it follows that we should not worry too much about shorter-term fluctuations in share prices. All sorts of factors produce share price swings, some based on economic reality and others on prevailing stock market sentiment, but in the longer term companies with strong fundamentals will always rise to the surface.

Dividend growth is the most important factor in deciding which shares rise furthest.

5. Read the report and accounts

Check whether sales and profits are rising and whether cash is flowing in or out of the business. See if the dividend is rising year by year and whether it is well covered by profits. Look at the gearing and ascertain whether interest payments are well covered by earnings.

6. Bear in mind total returns

If you are investing now for an income stream some time in the future, say for retirement, you can build your portfolio patiently for the long term rather than look for quick gains.

The most lucrative investments for the long term are those that combine capital gains with reinvested dividends. It is true that we are not concerned primarily with rising share prices but the total value of your portfolio is important if you do not want to draw on your income yet.

7. Reduce your tax burden

Make the most of your ISA and Self-invested personal pension (SIPP) entitlements. There is no obligation to pay tax on your earnings when you can easily and legitimately avoid making further contributions to the chancellor.

You cannot avoid paying standard rate tax on your dividends but most serious investors are likely to find themselves in a higher tax bracket.

However, do not invest just to use up your full tax entitlement for the financial year.

8. Avoid fashionable sectors

When everyone is piling into a particular sector, share prices are going to become inflated and yields will be squashed. While a sector may be popular because it genuinely offers the best growth prospects, you should stop to consider whether expectations are realistic. One only has to mention the dotcom boom and bust at the turn of the millennium to make the point.

Before that there was a boom and bust in biotech stocks, although with a less dramatic effect.

Fashionable investments often carry the promise of dividends in the future rather than jam today. Even though you are taking a long-term view it is wise to look for shares that offer a pay back now.

9. Don't be greedy

While we are naturally looking for shares that offer attractive rewards, we should not blindly pile into companies with excessively high yields. Such companies are seen as high risk. It is possible that they have been high-growth stocks in markets that are now saturated.

Beware of companies with yields that are more than twice as high as the FTSE 100 average; those where the dividend has remained flat for several years; and those with a high level of debt.

10. Take AIM with care

The Alternative Investment Market is not a great place for dividend investors. Most AIM companies do not pay dividends – indeed many do not make a profit in any given year.

AIM-quoted shares cannot be included in an ISA and although most are exempt from inheritance tax, that concession is likely to be of little interest to investors whose first priority is a stream of income now.

APPENDIX

Dividend Data for FTSE 350 Companies

The following table gives dividend data for the FTSE 350 companies as of 3 February 2012.

Company	TIDM	Subsector	Dividend (p)	Yield	Dividend cover
3i Group	III	Specialty Finance	3.6	1.9	5.4
3i Infrastructure Ltd	3IN	Equity Investment Instruments	5.72	4.7	2.0
Aberdeen Asset Management	ADN	Asset Managers	9	3.6	1.7
Aberforth Smaller Companies Trust	ASL	Equity Investment Instruments	20.75	3.5	1.2
Admiral Group	ADM	Insurance Brokers	32.4	3.4	2.2
Aegis Group	AGS	Media Agencies	2.6757	1.7	2.4
Afren	AFR	Exploration & Production			
African Barrick Gold Ltd	ABG	Gold Mining	3.29	0.6	10.7
Aggreko	AGK	Business Support Services	19.5097	0.9	4.1
Alliance Trust	ATST	Equity Investment Instruments	8.395	2.3	1.0
Allied Gold Mining	ALD	Gold Mining			
AMEC	AMEC	Oil Equipment & Services	26.5	2.6	2.2
Amlin	AML	Property & Casualty Insurance	23	6.8	2.1
Anglo American	AAL	General Mining	40.481	1.4	6.1
Anglo Pacific Group	APF	General Mining	9.05	3.0	1.6
Antofagasta	ANTO	General Mining	10.232	0.8	6.6
Aquarius Platinum Ltd	AQP	Platinum & Precious Metals	4.95	2.9	3.8
ARM Holdings	ARM	Semiconductors	3.48	0.6	2.4
Ashmore Group	ASHM	Asset Managers	14.5	3.8	1.8
Ashtead Group	AHT	Business Support Services	3	1.2	1.1
Associated British Foods	ABF	Food Products	24.75	2.1	2.8
AstraZeneca	AZN	Pharmaceuticals	161.6	5.4	2.6
Atkins (W S)	ATK	Business Support Services	29	4.0	2.7

Company	TIDM	Subsector	Dividend (p)	Yield	Dividend cover
AVEVA Group	AVV	Software	18.25	1.1	2.9
Aviva	AV.	Life Insurance	25.5	7.0	2.6
AZ Electronic Materials SA	AZEM	Specialty Chemicals			
Babcock International Group	BAB	Business Support Services	19.4	2.6	1.5
BAE Systems	BA.	Defence	17.5	5.6	2.3
Balfour Beatty	BBY	Heavy Construction	12.7	4.5	2.2
Bankers Investment Trust	BNKR	Equity Investment Instruments	12.7	3.2	0.9
Barclays	BARC	Banks	5.5	2.4	3.9
Barr (A G)	BAG	Soft Drinks	25.41	2.0	2.3
Barratt Developments	BDEV	Home Construction			
BBA Aviation	BBA	Transportation Services	8.1	4.3	1.9
Beazley	BEZ	Property & Casualty Insurance	7.5	5.2	3.5
Bellway	BWY	Home Construction	12.5	1.6	3.3
Berendsen	BRSN	Business Support Services	21.2	4.5	1.4
Berkeley Group Holdings (The)	BKG	Home Construction			
Betfair Group	BET	Gambling	5.9	0.7	6.3
BG Group	BG.	Integrated Oil & Gas	13.66	1.0	5.5
BH Global Ltd	BHGG	Equity Investment Instruments			
BH Macro Ltd	BHMU	Equity Investment Instruments			
BHP Billiton	BLT	General Mining	63.192	2.9	4.3
Big Yellow Group	BYG	Specialty REITs	9	3.1	1.8
BlackRock World Mining Trust	BRWM	Equity Investment Instruments	6	0.8	1.1
Bluecrest Allblue Fund Ltd	BABS	Equity Investment Instruments			

Company	TIDM	Subsector	Dividend (p)	Yield	Dividend cover
Bodycote	BOY	Industrial Machinery	8.7	2.7	2.1
Booker Group	BOK	Food Retailers & Wholesalers	1.67	2.3	2.3
Bovis Homes Group	BVS	Home Construction	3	0.6	3.7
BP	BP.	Integrated Oil & Gas	4.337	0.9	-6.4
Brewin Dolphin Holdings	BRW	Asset Managers	7.1	4.6	1.2
British American Tobacco	BATS	Tobacco	114.2	3.8	1.5
British Assets Trust	BSET	Equity Investment Instruments	6.112	4.9	0.9
British Empire Securities & General Trust	BTEM	Equity Investment Instruments	8.5	1.9	1.4
British Land Co	BLND	Retail REITs	26	5.3	1.2
British Sky Broadcasting Group	BSY	Broadcasting & Entertainment	23.28	3.4	1.8
Britvic	BVIC	Soft Drinks	17.7	4.9	1.8
Brown (N) Group	BWNG	Apparel Retailers	12.41	5.3	2.1
BT Group	BT.A	Fixed Line Telecommunications	7.4	3.6	2.5
BTG	BGC	Biotechnology			
Bumi	BUMI	Coal			
Bunzl	BNZL	Business Support Services	23.35	2.7	2.2
Burberry Group	BRBY	Clothing & Accessories	20	1.4	2.4
Bwin.Party Digital Entertainment	BPTY	Gambling			
Cable & Wireless Communications	CWC	Fixed Line Telecommunications	4.99	11.5	0.8
Cable & Wireless Worldwide	CW.	Fixed Line Telecommunications	4.5	21.6	1.9
Cairn Energy	CNE	Exploration & Production			
Caledonia Investments	CLDN	Equity Investment Instruments	37.1	2.5	3.2
Cape	CIU	Oil Equipment & Services	12	2.8	3.4

Company	TIDM	Subsector	Dividend (p)	Yield	Dividend cover
Capita Group (The)	CPI	Business Support Services	20	3.2	1.9
Capital & Counties Properties	CAPC	Real Estate Holding & Development	1.5	0.8	14.7
Capital Shopping Centres Group	CSCG	Retail REITs	15	4.5	-0.2
Carillion	CLLN	Business Support Services	15.5	4.9	2.2
Carnival	CCL	Recreational Services	61.928	3.2	2.5
Carpetright	CPR	Home Improvement Retailers	8	1.3	2.8
Catlin Group Ltd	CGL	Property & Casualty Insurance	26.5	6.3	2.2
Centamin Egypt Ltd	CEY	Gold Mining			
Centrica	CNA	Gas Distribution	14.3	4.8	3.0
Chemring Group	CHG	Defene	14.8	3.7	2.7
City of London Investment Trust (The)	CTY	Equity Investment Instruments	13.2	4.5	1.0
Close Brothers Group	CBG	Investment Services	40	5.7	1.0
Cobham	COB	Aerospace	6	3.2	2.9
COLT Group SA	COLT	Fixed Line Telecommunications			
Compass Group	CPG	Restaurants & Bars	19.3	3.2	2.0
Computacenter	CCC	Computer Services	13.2	3.2	2.5
Cookson Group	CKSN	Diversified Industrials	11.5	1.9	4.9
Cranswick	CWK	Food Products	27.5	3.5	2.7
CRH	CRH	Building Materials & Fixtures	40.3278	3.2	1.5
Croda International	CRDA	Specialty Chemicals	35	1.8	2.7
CSR	CSR	Telecommunications Equipment	4	1.7	7.0
Daejan Holdings	DJAN	Real Estate Holding & Development	75	2.5	5.5
Daily Mail and General Trust	DMGT	Publishing	17	3.7	2.5

Company	TIDM	Subsector	Dividend (p)	Yield	Dividend cover
Dairy Crest Group	DCG	Food Products	19.7	6.2	2.1
De La Rue	DLAR	Business Support Services	42.3	4.4	-0.1
Debenhams	DEB	Broad Line Retailers	3	4.3	3.0
Derwent London	DLN	Industrial & Office REITs	29	1.7	1.5
Devro	DVO	Food Products	7	2.5	2.5
Dexion Absolute Ltd	DAB	Equity Investment Instruments			
Diageo	DGE	Distillers & Vintners	40.4	2.8	2.2
Dignity	DTY	Specialised Consumer Services	8.88	1.1	5.3
Diploma	DPLM	Industrial Suppliers	12	3.0	2.0
Dixons Retail	DXNS	Specialty Retailers			
Domino Printing Sciences	DNO	Electronic Equipment	18.75	3.1	2.0
Domino's Pizza UK & IRL	DOM	Restaurants & Bars	10.2	2.2	1.6
Drax Group	DRX	Conventional Electricity	32	5.9	1.6
Dunelm Group	DNLM	Home Improvement Retailers	11.5	2.5	2.6
easyJet	EZJ	Airlines	10.5	2.3	4.6
Edinburgh Dragon Trust	EFM	Equity Investment Instruments	3.2	1.3	1.3
Edinburgh Investment Trust (The)	EDIN	Equity Investment Instruments	10	2.1	
Electra Private Equity	ELTA	Equity Investment Instruments			
Electrocomponents	ECM	Industrial Suppliers	11.5	4.9	1.5
Elementis	ELM	Specialty Chemicals	3.1	2.0	3.1
EnQuest	ENQ	Exploration & Production			
Essar Energy	ESSR	Renewable Energy Equipment			
Eurasian Natural Resources Corporation	ENRC	General Mining	19.471	2.8	4.9

Company	TIDM	Subsector	Dividend (p)	Yield	Dividend cover
Euromoney Institutional Investor	ERM	Publishing	18.75	2.7	2.1
Evraz	EVR	Iron & Steel			
Exillon Energy	EXI	Exploration & Production			
Experian	EXPN	Business Support Services	17.684	2.0	1.8
F&C Asset Management	FCAM	Asset Managers	3	4.4	-0.3
F&C Commercial Property Trust Ltd	FCPT	Industrial & Office REITs	6	5.8	2.6
Fenner	FENR	Industrial Machinery	8	1.7	3.1
Ferrexpo	FXPO	Iron & Steel	4.314	1.2	10.8
Fidelity China Special Situation	FCSS	Equity Investment Instruments	0.25	0.3	1.9
Fidelity European Values	FEV	Equity Investment Instruments	15.75	1.5	1.0
Fidessa Group	FDSA	Software	33	2.0	2.1
Filtrona	FLTR	Industrial Suppliers	9	2.3	2.3
FirstGroup	FGP	Travel & Tourism	22.12	7.2	2.1
Foreign & Colonial Investment Trust	FRCL	Equity Investment Instruments	6.75	2.3	0.8
Fresnillo	FRES	Platinum & Precious Metals	39.395	1.5	2.1
G4S	GFS	Business Support Services	7.9	2.9	1.8
Galliford Try	GFRD	Heavy Construction	16	3.3	1.9
Gem Diamonds Ltd	GEMD	Diamonds & Gemstones			
Genesis Emerging Markets Fund Ltd	GSS	Non equity Investment Instruments			
Genus	GNS	Biotechnology	13.3	1.3	3.5
GKN	GKN	Auto Parts	5	2.3	3.6
GlaxoSmithKline	GSK	Pharmaceuticals	65	4.7	0.9
Glencore International	GLEN	General Mining			

Company	TIDM	Subsector	Dividend (p)	Yield	Dividend cover
Go-Ahead Group (The)	GOG	Travel & Tourism	81	6.4	1.7
Grainger	GRI	Real Estate Holding & Development	1.3	1.3	5.1
Great Portland Estates	GPOR	Industrial & Office REITs	8.2	2.3	3.1
Greene King	GNK	Restaurants & Bars	23.1	4.6	2.4
Greggs	GRG	Food Retailers & Wholesalers	18.2	3.5	2.1
Halfords Group	HFD	Specialty Retailers	22	6.7	1.9
Halma	HLMA	Electronic Equipment	9.1	2.5	2.1
Hammerson	HMSO	Retail REITs	15.95	4.2	1.2
Hansteen Holdings	HSTN	Real Estate Holding & Development	3.4483	4.7	1.3
Hargreaves Lansdown	HL.	Asset Managers	12.91	3.0	1.6
Hays	HAS	Business Training & Employment Agencies	5.8	7.3	0.9
Henderson Group	HGG	Asset Managers	6.5	5.6	1.4
Herald Investment Trust	HRI	Equity Investment Instruments			
Heritage Oil Ltd	HOIL	Exploration & Production			
HICL Infrastructure Company Ltd	HICL	Equity Investment Instruments	6.7	5.7	0.7
Hikma Pharmaceuticals	HIK	Pharmaceuticals	8.2	1.2	4.2
Hiscox Ltd	HSX	Property & Casualty Insurance	16.5	4.3	2.7
Hochschild Mining	HOC	General Mining	3.136	0.6	7.0
Home Retail Group	HOME	Broad Line Retailers	14.7	13.3	1.5
Homeserve	HSV	Business Support Services	10.3	3.6	2.3
Howden Joinery Group	HWDN	Industrial Suppliers			
HSBC Holdings	HSBA	Banks	22.738	4.2	0.5
Hunting	HTG	Oil Equipment & Services	12	1.4	2.3

Company	TIDM	Subsector	Dividend (p)	Yield	Dividend cover
ICAP	IAP	Investment Services	19.95	5.2	1.7
IG Group Holdings	IGG	Investment Services	20	4.1	1.8
Imagination Technologies Group	IMG	Semiconductors			
IMI	IMI	Industrial Machinery	26	2.9	2.5
Impax Environmental Markets	IEM	Equity Investment Instruments	0.75	0.8	1.1
Imperial Tobacco Group	IMT	Tobacco	95.1	4.1	1.9
Inchcape	INCH	Specialty Retailers	6.6	1.9	4.8
Informa	INF	Publishing	14	3.5	1.3
Inmarsat	ISAT	Mobile Telecommunications	23.85	5.9	1.5
InterContinental Hotels Group	IHG	Hotels	30	2.3	2.0
Intermediate Capital Group	ICP	Specialty Finance	18	6.1	2.2
International Consolidated Airlines Group SA	IAG	Airlines			
International Personal Finance	IPF	Consumer Finance	6.27	3.1	3.5
International Power	IPR	Multi-utilities	10.91	3.2	2.0
International Public Partnership Ltd	INPP	Equity Investment Instruments	5.6934	4.7	0.6
Interserve	IRV	Business Support Services	18	6.1	1.6
Intertek Group	ITRK	Business Support Services	28.1	1.3	3.0
Invensys	ISYS	Software	4	2.0	6.3
Investec	INVP	Investment Services	17	4.2	2.4
ITE Group	ITE	Media Agencies	6.1	2.7	2.2
ITV	ITV	Broadcasting & Entertainment			
Jardine Lloyd Thompson Group	JLT	Insurance Brokers	22.5	3.3	2.1
JD Sports Fashion	JD.	Apparel Retailers	23	3.1	5.3

Company	TIDM	Subsector	Dividend (p)	Yield	Dividend cover
John Laing Infrastructure Fund Ltd	JLIF	Equity Investment Instruments	0.4972	0.5	10.4
John Wood Group	WG.	Oil Equipment & Services	9.072	1.4	3.2
Johnson Matthey	JMAT	Specialty Chemicals	46	2.1	2.6
JPMorgan American Investment Trust	JAM	Equity Investment Instruments	11	1.2	1.0
JPMorgan Asian Investment Trust	JAI	Equity Investment Instruments	2.2	1.1	1.0
JPMorgan Emerging Markets Inv Trust	JMG	Equity Investment Instruments	3.5	0.6	1.6
JPMorgan European Smaller Companies Trust	JESC	Equity Investment Instruments	4	0.6	1.3
JPMorgan Indian Investment Trust	JII	Equity Investment Instruments			
JPMorgan Russian Securities	JRS	Equity Investment Instruments			
Jupiter Fund Management	JUP	Asset Managers	4.7	2.0	3.3
Kazakhmys	KAZ	General Mining	13.749	1.2	12.6
KCOM Group	KCOM	Fixed Line Telecommunications	3.6	4.9	1.6
Kenmare Resources	KMR	General Mining			
Kentz Corporation Ltd	KENZ	Oil Equipment & Services	6.476	1.4	3.9
Kesa Electricals	KESA	Specialty Retailers	6.125	8.7	2.1
Kier Group	KIE	Heavy Construction	64	4.6	1.8
Kingfisher	KGF	Home Improvement Retailers	7.07	2.6	3.1
Ladbrokes	LAD	Gambling	7.6	5.3	5.7
Laird	LRD	Electrical Components & Equipment	6.3	3.7	1.2
Lamprell	LAM	Oil Equipment & Services	7.563	2.3	1.7
Lancashire Holdings Ltd	LRE	Property & Casualty Insurance	9.55	1.3	12.4
Land Securities Group	LAND	Industrial & Office REITs	28.2	4.2	1.7
Law Debenture Corporation (The)	LWDB	Equity Investment Instruments	12.7	3.5	1.0

Company	TIDM	Subsector	Dividend (p)	Yield	Dividend cover
Legal & General Group	LGEN	Life Insurance	4.75	4.0	3.0
Lloyds Banking Group	LLOY	Banks			
Logica	LOG	Computer Services	4.2	5.4	3.1
London & Stamford Property Ltd	LSP	Real Estate Holding & Development	6.3	5.9	2.0
London Stock Exchange Group	LSE	Investment Services	26.8	2.9	2.4
Lonmin	LMI	Platinum & Precious Metals	9.64	0.9	9.1
Man Group	EMG	Asset Managers	13.59	10.7	1.3
Marks & Spencer Group	MKS	Broad Line Retailers	17	5.1	2.3
Marston's	MARS	Restaurants & Bars	5.8	5.9	1.9
Meggitt	MGGT	Aerospace	9.2	2.5	2.4
Melrose	MRO	Industrial Machinery	10.6335	2.8	2.3
Mercantile Investment Trust (The)	MRC	Equity Investment Instruments	36	3.7	0.7
Merchants Trust (The)	MRCH	Equity Investment Instruments	22.8	6.1	0.9
Michael Page International	MPI	Business Training & Employment Agencies	9	2.1	1.1
Micro Focus International	MCRO	Software	14.793	3.3	2.2
Millennium & Copthorne Hotels	MLC	Hotels	10	2.2	3.6
Misys	MSY	Software			
Mitchells & Butlers	MAB	Restaurants & Bars			
MITIE Group	MTO	Business Support Services	9	3.5	2.3
Mondi	MNDI	Paper	17.485	3.3	2.3
Moneysupermarket.com Group	MONY	Media Agencies	3.83	3.2	0.3
Monks Investment Trust (The)	MNKS	Equity Investment Instruments	3	0.9	1.4
Morgan Crucible Company (The)	MGCR	Electrical Components & Equipment	7.7	2.4	2.3

Company	TIDM	Subsector	Dividend (p)	Yield	Dividend cover
Morrison (Wm) Supermarkets	MRW	Food Retailers & Wholesalers	9.6	3.4	2.4
Murray Income Trust	MUT	Equity Investment Instruments	28.75	4.5	1.1
Murray International Trust	MYI	Equity Investment Instruments	32	3.3	1.2
National Express Group	NEX	Travel & Tourism	6	2.7	3.3
National Grid	NG.	Multi-utilities	36.37	5.8	1.8
New World Resources	NWR	Coal	37.14	7.5	1.2
Next	NXT	Apparel Retailers	78	2.9	2.8
Northgate	NTG	Commercial Vehicles & Trucks			
Ocado Group	OCDO	Food Retailers & Wholesalers			
Old Mutual	OML	Life Insurance	4	2.6	2.0
Ophir Energy	OPHR	Exploration & Production			
Oxford Instruments	OXIG	Electronic Equipment	9	1.0	6.3
Paragon Group of Companies (The)	PAG	Consumer Finance	4	2.2	6.9
PayPoint	PAY	Financial Administration	23.4	4.0	1.5
Pearson	PSON	Publishing	38.7	3.2	1.8
Pennon Group	PNN	Water	24.65	3.6	1.7
Perform Group	PER	Broadcasting & Entertainment			
Perpetual Income & Growth Investment Trust	PLI	Equity Investment Instruments	9.35	3.6	1.1
Persimmon	PSN	Home Construction	7.5	1.4	5.6
Personal Assets Trust	PNL	Equity Investment Instruments	555	1.6	
Petrofac Ltd	PFC	Oil Equipment & Services	27.33	1.8	2.9
Petropavlovsk	POG	Gold Mining	10	1.2	2.9
Phoenix Group Holdings	PHNX	Life Insurance	42	7.1	3.0

Company	TIDM	Subsector	Dividend (p)	Yield	Dividend cover
Polar Capital Technology Trust	PCT	Equity Investment Instruments			
Polymetal Internetional	POLY	General Mining			
Premier Farnell	PFL	Industrial Suppliers	10.4	4.8	1.7
Premier Oil	PMO	Exploration & Production			
Provident Financial	PFG	Consumer Finance	63.5	6.4	1.2
Prudential	PRU	Life Insurance	23.85	3.3	2.4
PZ Cussons	PZC	Personal Products	6.61	2.1	2.4
QinetiQ Group	QQ.	Defence	1.6	1.2	4.4
Randgold Resources Ltd	RRS	Gold Mining	12.774	0.2	4.6
Rank Group (The)	RNK	Gambling	2.4	1.7	7.4
Rathbone Brothers	RAT	Asset Managers	44	3.7	1.1
Reckitt Benckiser Group	RB.	Non-durable Household Products	115	3.4	1.9
Redrow	RDW	Home Construction			
Reed Elsevier	REL	Publishing	20.4	3.9	1.6
Regus	RGU	Business Support Services	2.6	2.5	0.8
Renishaw	RSW	Electronic Equipment	35	2.4	2.5
Rentokil Initial	RTO	Business Support Services			
Resolution Ltd	RSL	Life Insurance	18.03	6.5	4.5
Restaurant Group (The)	RTN	Restaurants & Bars	9	3.0	2.3
Rexam	REX	Containers & Packaging	12	3.2	2.4
Rightmove	RMV	Media Agencies	14	1.1	2.5
Rio Tinto	RIO	General Mining	67.35	1.7	6.7
RIT Capital Partners	RCP	Equity Investment Instruments	4	0.3	0.9

Company	TIDM	Subsector	Dividend (p)	Yield	Dividend cover
Rolls-Royce Group	RR.	Aerospace	16	2.1	1.7
Rotork	ROR	Industrial Machinery	32.5	1.7	2.5
Royal Bank of Scotland Group (The)	RBS	Banks			
Royal Dutch Shell	RDSB	Integrated Oil & Gas	107.983	4.7	1.9
RPC Group	RPC	Containers & Packaging	10.813	2.8	3.1
RPS Group	RPS	Business Support Services	4.83	2.2	3.3
RSA Insurance Group	RSA	Full Line Insurance	8.82	8.0	1.1
SABMiller	SAB	Brewers	50.429	2.1	2.1
Sage Group (The)	SGE	Software	9.75	3.3	2.0
Sainsbury (J)	SBRY	Food Retailers & Wholesalers	15.1	5.2	1.9
Salamander Energy	SMDR	Exploration & Production			
Savills	SVS	Real Estate Services	13	3.6	1.8
Schroders	SDR	Asset Managers	37	2.3	2.9
Scottish Investment Trust	SCIN	Equity Investment Instruments	10.4	2.2	1.2
Scottish Mortgage Investment Trust	SMT	Equity Investment Instruments	12	1.8	1.1
SDL	SDL	Software	5.5	0.8	5.0
Segro	SGRO	Industrial & Office REITs	14.3	6.4	1.5
Senior	SNR	Aerospace	3.12	1.7	3.5
Serco Group	SRP	Business Support Services	7.35	1.4	4.4
Severn Trent	SVT	Water	65.09	4.3	1.4
Shaftesbury	SHB	Retail REITs	11.25	2.2	0.1
Shanks Group	SKS	Waste & Disposal Services	3.25	2.9	1.3
Shire	SHP	Pharmaceuticals	8.14	0.4	9.1

Company	TIDM	Subsector	Dividend (p)	Yield	Dividend cover
SIG	SHI	Industrial Suppliers			
Smith & Nephew	SN.	Medical Equipment	9.785	1.5	4.7
Smith (DS)	SMDS	Containers & Packaging	6.5	2.9	2.5
Smiths Group	SMIN	Diversified Industrials	36.25	3.8	2.4
SOCO International	SIA	Exploration & Production			
Spectris	SXS	Electrical Components & Equipment	28	1.7	3.0
Spirax-Sarco Engineering	SPX	Industrial Machinery	43	2.1	2.7
Spirent Communications	SPT	Telecommunications Equipment	1.55	1.2	4.8
Sports Direct International	SPD	Apparel Retailers			
SSE	SSE	Conventional Electricity	75	6.1	3.0
St James's Place	STJ	Life Insurance	6	1.6	1.9
Stagecoach Group	SGC	Travel & Tourism	7.2032	2.6	3.2
Standard Chartered	STAN	Banks	43.972	2.8	2.8
Standard Life	SL.	Life Insurance	13	5.8	1.6
Stobart Group Ltd	STOB	Transportation Services	6	4.7	1.5
SuperGroup	SGP	Clothing & Accessories			
SVG Capital	SVI	Equity Investment Instruments			
Synergy Health	SYR	Health Care Providers	15.84	1.8	2.6
TalkTalk Telecom Group	TALK	Fixed Line Telecommunications	5.6	4.6	1.8
Talvivaara Mining Company Ltd	TALV	Nonferrous Metals			
Tate & Lyle	TATE	Food Products	23.7	3.5	1.8
Taylor Wimpey	TW.	Home Construction			
Telecity Group	TCY	Computer Services			
Telecom plus	TEP	Fixed Line Telecommunications	22	3.2	1.4
Temple Bar Investment Trust	TMPL	Equity Investment Instruments	34.2	3.8	0.9

Company	TIDM	Subsector	Dividend (p)	Yield	Dividend cover
Templeton Emerging Markets Inv Tr	TEM	Equity Investment Instruments	4.25	0.7	1.4
Tesco	TSCO	Food Retailers & Wholesalers	14.46	4.5	1.9
TR Property Investment Trust	TRY	Equity Investment Instruments	6	3.8	1.2
Travis Perkins	TPK	Industrial Suppliers	15	1.6	4.7
TUI Travel	TT.	Travel & Tourism	11.3	5.7	1.5
Tullett Prebon	TLPR	Investment Services	15.75	5.0	3.2
Tullow Oil	TLW	Exploration & Production	6	0.4	2.6
UBM	UBM	Publishing	25	4.4	1.6
UK Commercial Property Trust Ltd	UKCM	Industrial & Office REITs	5.252	7.1	1.5
Ultra Electronics Holdings	ULE	Defence	34.6	2.2	2.8
Unilever	ULVR	Food Products	71.24	3.6	1.9
UNITE Group	UTG	Real Estate Holding & Development			
United Utilities Group	UU.	Water	30	5.1	1.4
Vedanta Resources	VED	General Mining	32.03	2.4	6.3
Victrex	VCT	Specialty Chemicals	32.5	2.4	2.6
Vodafone Group	VOD	Mobile Telecommunications	8.9	5.2	2.4
Weir Group	WEIR	Industrial Machinery	27	1.3	3.5
Wetherspoon (J D)	JDW	Restaurants & Bars	12	2.9	2.9
WH Smith	SMWH	Specialty Retailers	22.5	4.2	2.2
Whitbread	WTB	Restaurants & Bars	44.5	2.7	2.8
William Hill	WMH	Gambling	8.3	3.6	2.3
Witan Investment Trust	WTAN	Equity Investment Instruments	10.9	2.3	0.9
Wolseley	WOS	Industrial Suppliers	45	2.0	2.8
WPP Group	WPP	Media Agencies	17.79	2.3	2.8
Xstrata	XTA	General Mining	16.116	1.3	6.9
Yule Catto & Co	YULC	Specialty Chemicals	2.6	1.3	7.0

Index

D

Dow Jones Industrial Average (DJIA) 215, 216

DRIPs (dividend reinvestment plans) 12-13

Dudley, Bob 240-1, 243

due diligence 171

E

EBIT (earnings before interest and tax) 105

Eddie Stobart (haulage company) 164-6

engineering sector 194, 201

EPS (earnings per share) ratio 92-6, 99, 102, 209

ethical investing 177-9

Eurotunnel (travel company) 188-9

ex-dividend dates 21-3, 25, 39

expanding operations 140

F

fashionable sectors 247

final dividends

and AGMs 7, 9

distribution of 26-7

and half-year results statements 54

and historic dividend yield 84

payment frequency 18-19

restoring 155

and result announcements 37, 40-1

weighting of 19-20

finance directors 8-9, 11, 15, 37, 94

Financial Express (independent statistics firm) 177

financial spread betting 43

Financial Times (newspaper) 33, 99, 193

financial websites 31-2, 86-7, 206-14

financial year

AGMs 53

and half-year results statement 54-6

outlook statements 51, 58-9

results issued 52

trading summaries 49-51, 59-60

trading updates 49-50, 53-4, 57-9

First Student (US school bus service) 54

First Transit (US bus service) 54

FirstGroup (transport company) 49-60

five year financial summaries 41-2, 63-5

flotations 139-42

forecasting yields 85-7

foreign companies 192

foreign currency 14-15, 192-3, 214

four-times-a-year payments 18-19, 41, 81

free cash flow 110

FTSE companies

cash flow 109

dividend cover 101

dividend data 251-65

dividend histories 72-4

dividend yields 81-3, 88-9

dividend-paying profiles 127-9

and 'Dogs of the Dow' system 217

EPS ratios 93

and ethical investing 177

and ex-dividend dates 22

and interest cover 106-7

S